THE PELICAN SHAKESPEARE

GENERAL EDITOR : ALFRED HARBAGE

AB27

LOVE'S LABOR'S LOST

# WILLIAM SHAKESPEARE

# Love's Labor's Lost

### EDITED BY ALFRED HARBAGE

PENGUIN BOOKS
BALTIMORE · MARYLAND

This edition first published 1963
Penguin Books Inc.
3300 Clipper Mill Road, Baltimore 11, Maryland

Library of Congress Catalog Card
Number 62-7709

*Printed in the United States of America*

# CONTENTS

# CONTENTS

# SHAKESPEARE AND HIS STAGE

William Shakespeare was christened in Holy Trinity Church, Stratford-on-Avon, April 26, 1564. His birth is traditionally assigned to April 23rd. He was the eldest of four boys and two girls who survived infancy in the family of John Shakespeare, glover and trader of Henley Street, and his wife Mary Arden, daughter of a small landowner of Wilmcote. In 1568 John was elected Bailiff (equivalent to Mayor) of Stratford, having already filled the minor municipal offices. The town maintained for the sons of the burgesses a free school, taught by a university graduate and offering preparation in Latin sufficient for university entrance; its early registers are lost, but there can be little doubt that Shakespeare received the formal part of his education in this school.

On November 27, 1582, a license was issued for the marriage of William Shakespeare (aged eighteen) and Ann Hathaway (aged twenty-six), and on May 26, 1583, their child Susanna was christened in Holy Trinity Church. The inference that the marriage was forced upon the youth is natural but not inevitable; betrothal was legally binding at the time, and was sometimes regarded as conferring conjugal rights. Two additional children of the marriage, the twins Hamnet and Judith, were christened on February 2, 1585. Meanwhile the prosperity of the elder Shakespeares had declined, and William was impelled to seek a career outside Stratford.

The tradition that he spent some time as a country teacher is old but unverifiable. Because of the absence of records his early twenties are called the "lost years," and only one thing about them is certain — that at least some of these years were spent in winning a place in the acting profession. He may have begun as a provincial trouper, but by 1592 he was established in London and prominent enough to be attacked. In a pamphlet of that year, *Groatsworth of Wit*, the ailing Robert Greene complained of the neglect which university writers like himself had suffered from actors, one of whom was daring to set up as a playwright:

> ... an upstart crow beautified with our feathers, that with his *Tiger's heart wrapt in a player's hide* supposes he is as well able to bombast out a blank verse as the best of you, and being an absolute Johannes-factotum, is in his own conceit the only Shake-scene in a country.

The pun on his name, and the parody of his line "O tiger's heart wrapt in a woman's hide" (*III Henry VI*), pointed clearly to Shakespeare. Some of his admirers protested, and Henry Chettle, the editor of Greene's pamphlet, saw fit to apologize:

> I am as sorry as if the original fault had been my fault, because myself have seen his demeanor no less civil than he excellent in the quality he professes. Besides divers of worship have reported his uprightness of dealing, which argues his honesty, and his facetious grace in writing that approves his art. (Prefatory epistle, *Kind Heart's Dream*)

The plague closed the London theatres for many months in 1593–94, denying the actors their livelihood. To this period belong Shakespeare's two narrative poems, *Venus and Adonis* and *Rape of Lucrece*, both dedicated to the Earl of Southampton. No doubt the poet was rewarded with a gift of money as usual in such cases, but he did no further dedicating and we have no reliable information on whether Southampton, or anyone else, became his regular patron. His sonnets, first mentioned in 1598 and published without his consent in 1609, are intimate without being explicitly autobiographical. They seem to commemorate the poet's friendship with an idealized youth, rivalry with a more favored poet, and love affair with a dark mistress; and his bitterness when the mistress betrays him in conjunction with the friend; but it is difficult to decide precisely what the "story" is, impossible to decide whether it is fictional or true. The real distinction of the sonnets, at least of those not purely conventional, rests in the universality of the thoughts and moods they express, and in their poignancy and beauty.

In 1594 was formed the theatrical company known until 1603 as the Lord Chamberlain's Men, thereafter as the King's Men. Its original membership included, besides Shakespeare, the beloved clown Will Kempe and the famous actor Richard Burbage. The company acted in various London theatres and even toured the provinces, but it is chiefly associated in our minds with the Globe Theatre built on the south bank of the Thames in 1599. Shakespeare was an actor and joint owner of this company (and its Globe) through the remainder of his creative years. His plays, written at the average rate of two a year, together with Burbage's acting won it its place of leadership among the London companies.

Individual plays began to appear in print, in editions both honest and piratical, and the publishers became increasingly aware of the value of Shakespeare's name on the title pages. As early as 1598 he was hailed as the leading English dramatist in the *Palladis Tamia* of Francis Meres:

9

As Plautus and Seneca are accounted the best for Comedy and Tragedy among the Latins, so Shakespeare among the English is the most excellent in both kinds for the stage: for Comedy, witness his *Gentlemen of Verona*, his *Errors*, his *Love labors lost*, his *Love labors won [Taming of the Shrew?]*, his *Midsummers night dream*, & his *Merchant of Venice*; for Tragedy, his *Richard the 2*, *Richard the 3*, *Henry the 4*, *King John*, *Titus Andronicus*, and his *Romeo and Juliet*.

The note is valuable, both in indicating Shakespeare's prestige and in helping us to establish a chronology. In the second half of his writing career, history plays gave place to the great tragedies; and farces and light comedies gave place to the problem plays and symbolic romances. In 1623, seven years after his death, his former fellow actors, John Hemming and Henry Condell, cooperated with a group of London printers in bringing out his plays in collected form. The volume is generally known as the First Folio.

Shakespeare had never severed his relations with Stratford. His wife and children may sometimes have shared his London lodgings, but their home was Stratford. His son Hamnet was buried there in 1596, and his daughters Susanna and Judith were married there in 1607 and 1616 respectively. (His father, for whom he had secured a coat of arms and thus the privilege of writing himself gentleman, died in 1601, his mother in 1608.) His considerable earnings in London, as actor-sharer, part owner of the Globe, and playwright, were invested chiefly in Stratford property. In 1597 he purchased for £60 New Place, one of the two most imposing residences in the town. A number of other business transactions, as well as minor episodes in his career, have left documentary records. By 1611 he was in a position to retire, and he seems gradually to have withdrawn from theatrical activity in order to live in Stratford. In March, 1616, he made a will, leaving token bequests to Burbage, Hemming, and Condell, but the bulk of his estate to his family. The most famous feature of the will, the bequest of the second-best bed to his wife, reveals nothing about Shakespeare's marriage; the quaintness of the provision seems commonplace to those familiar with ancient testaments. Shakespeare died April 23, 1616, and was buried in the Stratford church where he had been christened. Within seven years a monument was erected to his memory on the north wall of the chancel. Its portrait bust and the Droeshout engraving on the title page of the First Folio provide the only likenesses with an established claim to authenticity. The best verbal vignette was written by his rival Ben Jonson, the more impressive for being imbedded in a context mainly critical:

> ... I loved the man, and do honor his memory (on this side idolatry) as much as any. He was indeed honest, and of an open and free nature: he had an excellent fancy, brave notions, and gentle expressions. ... (*Timber or Discoveries*, c. 1623–30)

The reader of Shakespeare's plays is aided by a general knowledge of the way in which they were staged. The King's Men acquired a roofed and artificially lighted theatre only toward the close of Shakespeare's career, and then only for winter use. Nearly all his plays were designed for performance in such structures as the Globe — a three-tiered amphitheatre with a large rectangular platform extending to the center of its yard. The plays were staged by daylight, by large casts brilliantly costumed, but with only a minimum of properties, without scenery, and quite possibly without intermissions. There was a rear stage balcony for action "above," and a curtained rear recess for "discoveries" and other special effects, but by far the major portion of any play was enacted upon the projecting platform, with episode following episode in swift succession, and with shifts of time and place signaled the audience only by the momentary clearing of the stage between the episodes. Information about the identity of the characters and, when necessary, about the time and place of the action was incorporated in the dialogue. No additional indications of place have been inserted in the present editions; these are apt to obscure the original fluidity of structure, with the emphasis upon action and speech rather than scenic background. The acting, including that of the youthful apprentices to the profession who performed the parts of women, was highly skillful, with a premium placed upon grace of gesture and beauty of diction. The audiences, a cross section of the general public, commonly numbered a thousand, sometimes more than two thousand. Judged by the type of plays they applauded, these audiences were not only large but also perceptive.

## THE TEXTS OF THE PLAYS

About half of Shakespeare's plays appeared in print for the first time in the folio volume of 1623. The others had been published individually, usually in quarto volumes, during his lifetime or in the six years following his death. The copy used by the printers of the quartos varied greatly in merit, sometimes representing Shakespeare's true text, sometimes only a debased version of that text. The copy used by the printers of the folio also varied in merit, but was chosen with care. Since it consisted of the best available manuscripts, or the more acceptable quartos (although frequently in editions other than the first), or of quartos corrected by reference to manuscripts, we have good or reasonably good texts of most of the thirty-seven plays.

In the present series, the plays have been newly edited from quarto or folio texts depending, when a choice offered, upon which is now regarded by bibliographical specialists as the more authoritative. The ideal has been to reproduce the chosen texts with as few alterations as possible, beyond occasional relineation, expansion of abbreviations, and modernization of punctuation and spelling. Emendation is held to a minimum, and such material as has been added, in the way of stage directions and lines supplied by an alternative text, has been enclosed in square brackets.

None of the plays printed in Shakespeare's lifetime were divided into acts and scenes, and the inference is that the author's own manuscripts were not so divided. In the folio collection, some of the plays remained undivided, some were divided into acts, and some were divided into acts and scenes. During the eighteenth century all of the plays were divided into acts and scenes, and in the Cambridge edition of the mid-nineteenth century, from which the influential Globe text derived, this division was more or less regularized and the lines were numbered. Many useful works of reference employ the act-scene-line apparatus established by the Globe text.

Since the act-scene division thus established is obviously convenient, but is of very dubious authority so far as Shakespeare's own structural principles are concerned, or the original manner of staging his plays, a problem is presented to modern editors. In the present series the act-scene division of the Globe text is retained marginally, and may be viewed as a reference aid like the line numbering. A printer's ornament marks the points of division when these points have been determined by a cleared stage indicating a shift of time and place in the action of the play, or when no harm results from the editorial assumption that there is such a shift. However, at those points where the established division is clearly misleading — that is, where continuous action has been split up into separate "scenes" — the ornament is omitted and the distortion corrected. This mechanical expedient seemed the best means of combining utility and accuracy.

*The General Editor.*

# INTRODUCTION

To Tolstoy Shakespeare seemed a poet in motley, who was "only playing with words." If he felt this way about *Lear,* we can guess how he would have felt about *Love's Labor's Lost* had he been able to endure reading it. In a way Tolstoy was right. An irrepressible, almost irresponsible gaiety breaks through as verbal effervescence even in plays written when Shakespeare was allegedly in the depths, in scenes where other playwrights would have preserved a fitting decorum. Johnson noted the fact with temperate regret: word-play, the pun, the "clench" was the poet's "fatal Cleopatra." Since the Shakespeare of *Love's Labor's Lost* is visible in all his works, we can scarcely call the play uncharacteristic. It is quite characteristic of Shakespeare the virtuoso, the idea-juggler, the word-wright, who loved to play and, naturally, since it was his natural element, loved to play with language. The comedy is exceptional chiefly in this, that Tolstoy's word *only* is here almost applicable.

Before conceding its defects, we had better observe its merits, especially since they have languished in relative neglect until recent times. It is a mistake to suppose that the play is a kind of closet drama, offering its feast of language, "scraps" or otherwise, at the expense of effective action. On the contrary, it is excellent theatre and good — although delayed-action — drama. It has the tactical advantage of being built about a single acceptable idea, one that has become, if it was not so already, a situational cliché. Young men resolve to abstain from the society of young women until confronted with appealing young women, whereupon they break their resolution. What has to happen happens, to the gratification of the world which loves a lover. Shakespeare himself, here and in *Much Ado about Nothing,* may have been the first to exploit the "Benedick" theme, but an abundance of later literature demonstrates how eminently exploitable it was. Having grasped at once the basic idea, we watch its development in comfort. There are no teasing complications; each of the four young men falls patly in love with his opposite number. Interest is sustained less by the conjunction of episodes than by episodes in isolation, most of which could be played effectively as excerpts. Act IV, Scene iii, where each of the avowed celibates spies on the apostasy of his fellows, is a masterpiece of stage ingenuity, and the opening of Act V, Scene ii, where their temptresses wreck their "show of Muscovites," is full of irresistible business. The sketchy adventures of Armado, Moth, and the village eccentrics are just sufficient to float the interspersed series of comic dialogues, most of which could also be excerpted and played as vaudeville. Despite the absence of important action, the play is theatrically strong.

There is nothing reprehensible about word-play as such, and that of *Love's Labor's Lost* has the virtue of wholeheartedness. The language is energetic even at its most frivolous. Nearly every long speech is a verbal tumbling act, and every short one a stroke in a game of wits. Two-ply, three-ply, and four-ply puns ricochet from line to line, and if badness is the test of a good pun, some of these are immortal. All kinds of language affectation are exploited — genteelism, pedanticism, obscurantism, even poeticism:

16

Taffeta phrases, silken terms precise,
Three-piled hyperboles, spruce affection,
Figures pedantical. . . .

In his superior way Berowne is as much a linguistic fop as
Armado, while Holofernes commits matchless assaults
upon the Renaissance vocabulary. Even Jaquenetta's few
lines perform a supplementary function, supplying a
thumb-nail anthology of rustic comebacks of old, on the
level of the modern "sez you." The conceits of the semi-
serious passages are so complex and the comic puns so tenu-
ous that one wonders how much the audience was able to
catch. Probably a percentage only, although a larger one
than we might suppose. Actually, almost every line is ex-
plicable, even those which at first seem gibberish, but instant and total comprehension was scarcely necessary. A
listener could catch a share of the jokes and take the rest on
faith, exulting meanwhile in the power of the characters and
their creator to "keep it up."

The characterization is less impressive than the physical
and verbal movement, partly because most of the types presented were improved upon by Shakespeare himself in
other plays. The King of Navarre and the Princess of France
show a trace, but a trace only, of the royal grace and *savoir-
faire* of Theseus and Hippolyta. Rosaline has the pertness but
lacks the charm of Rosalind. Even Berowne is a little disap-
pointing: the rôle of giber-in-chief seems superimposed
upon him, as during his excessive and pointless denigration
of Boyet; he should have emerged more clearly as both the
most intelligent person in the play and the most intoxicated
by his own fluency. Perhaps when the play was written,
Shakespeare himself was too much of a Berowne to see the

character quite objectively. The other figures of the great world, Dumaine and Longaville, like Katharine and Maria, are so sketchy as to be scarcely distinguishable.

Among the low-comedy characters Dull is only a foreshadow of Dogberry, and Jaquenetta of Audrey. Costard is inferior to Shakespeare's later homespuns because he fails to stay in character. As the open-mouthed but dauntless simpleton he is fine, but he shifts sometimes into the smart-aleck and even the bawdy sophisticate. Armado and Moth, at least at the beginning, are bores absolute, and one pities the recluses for whom they are to provide "quick recreation" for three years; but Armado becomes interesting when he becomes pathetic, then heroic, and Moth when he acts in the show of Nine Worthies and becomes truly a boy. Of course the true comic triumphs are Holofernes and Nathaniel: Shakespeare never did better with pompous asininity and limp obsequiousness.

All of the characters have a speech or two in which they seem to excel themselves, and this brings us to an odd feature of the play — its extreme unevenness. The opening scene and a number more are written in fine blank verse and rime. The poetry is rarely of the highest Shakespearean order, often recalling the logic-chopping and intricate prettiness of the lesser Sonnets, but it is true poetry and written by a master prosodist. It ill prepares us for the old-fashioned doggerel we find elsewhere, descending sometimes to jingling triteness. Or compare the first dialogue of Armado and Moth (I, ii) with the first dialogue of Holofernes and Nathaniel (IV, ii), which despite its comparable thicket of verbiage has the breath of life in it.

There is disparity of tone as well as quality. Conspicuously at the end, and intermittently elsewhere, the bright brittle surface of the play seems to crack and reveal a warmer, gentler, more human substance — such as we associate with a more familiar Shakespeare, the humorist rather than the wit, the amused and affectionate observer rather than the gleeful satirist. Sometimes the play seems almost to protest against itself — as when its speakers resolve to "lay these glozes [i.e. double-talk] by" and praise "honest plain words," "russet yeas and honest kersey noes." The concluding speech rejects the harsh words of Mercury (master-glozer) for the songs of Apollo. Though harmless in intent, the play has truly its strain of harshness. It is admirable in its pioneering of the mode of social comedy, and the themes of warfare between the sexes and between naturalness and affectation, but like other pioneers it is often more rugged than refined, the postures of its characters too muscular, their persiflage too aggressive, indeed at times even brutal. Rosaline's words condemning the gibing spirit —

> A jest's prosperity lies in the ear
> Of him that hears it, never in the tongue
> Of him that makes it —

might as well have been directed at herself and all the other ladies and gentlemen as at Berowne alone. The impression is inescapable that the play has not only been revised, but revised after the author had considerably matured both as artist and individual, and found the spirit of the original piece not wholly to his taste.

The mere fact of revision is generally conceded. The problem is when it took place and why. The first edition in 1598, evidently printed from the author's manuscript, contains several duplicate passages, where the printer mistakenly preserved lines which had been cancelled and rewritten. These are of small help in deciding the main point, since such revision may take place either during the original composition or the reworking of a play. Also of small help is the information on the title page that the play had been "newly corrected and augmented," since the legend may only mean, as in the case of a similar one on the title page of the 1599 quarto of *Romeo and Juliet,* that there had been an earlier edition, unauthorized and unreliable. But the 1598 text of *Love's Labor's Lost,* the only authoritative one we have, shows signs of structural as well as stylistic revision, of shuffling about of speeches and speakers, and of an altered ending. It seems virtually certain that the play originally ended not with news of the death of the King of France, but with Boyet's production of the papers establishing the Princess's territorial claims. There is even a possibility that the suit of love succeeded as promptly as the suit of property, and that the original title was "Love's Labor's Won." A play with this title was attributed to Shakespeare by Francis Meres in 1598 along with *Love's Labor's Lost,* and a quarto so titled was extant in the early seventeenth century; however, the chances are somewhat in favor of its being a separate play rather than an earlier version of the one we have. There is no mention of either title before 1598, and the majority of present-day scholars believe that *Love's Labor's Lost* was originally written about 1594–95 in Shakespeare's "lyrical" period, and revised shortly before an event advertised on the title page, a performance at Elizabeth's court "this last Christmas" (probably that of 1596 or 1597).

It must be confessed that such a conclusion raises certain vexing questions: why was extensive revision necessary after so short a lapse of time? why does this particular play of the "lyrical" period contain patches of verse different from and inferior to anything else written by Shakespeare in the "lyrical" period? why should a play which seems to have been designed for a coterie audience have been performed by a popular troupe? The plays performed at Elizabeth's court in the 'nineties were all from the regular popular repertories, and the often repeated statement that *Love's Labor's Lost* was composed by a popular playwright for a private occasion rests on neither particular evidence nor general precedent but on strong and simple faith. One of the influences on the current dating has been the discussion of "topicalities" in the play. The earliest theory (1747) was Bishop Warburton's, that Holofernes was intended as a caricature of the busy translator and lexicographer John Florio. This theory has met with somewhat discriminatory disdain. The most prominent of more recent theories are that the Armado-Moth scenes make humorous capital of the personal quarrel between Thomas Nashe and Gabriel Harvey pursued in a series of notorious pamphlets in 1590–96, and that the fiction of a little "academe" with its courtly principals and orbiting eccentrics presents diffused satire of Royden, Raleigh, Harriot, Northumberland, Chapman, and other unorthodox thinkers who supposedly comprised an intellectual clique known as the "school of atheism," i.e. the "school of night" (cf. IV, iii, 250). A number of books and articles by reputable scholars have advanced these theories, which deserve the respectful attention they have received; however, none of them carries conviction except to those under the hypnosis induced by the shimmering nature of the evidence. A few suggestive phrases in the play there certainly are, but neither the characters nor the episodes resemble in the least the persons and events they are supposed to shadow forth.

There may be value in an alternate opinion on the date of original composition. Many generations of Shakespearean scholars believed *Love's Labor's Lost* to be Shakespeare's earliest play, and the more factual findings of modern scholarship have done nothing to discredit this belief. Although the plot is evidently original, a number of "sources" or ingredients have been discovered, and these are such as we would expect in a play of the late 'eighties rather than the middle 'nineties. The idea of a courtly philosophic retreat intruded upon by fetching ladies seems to have been suggested by an actual embassy to Henry of Navarre at Nerac by Marguerite de Valois, Catherine de Medici, and "l'escadron volant" of ladies-in-waiting in 1578. "Academies" were more in the news in the 'eighties than in the 'nineties; a suggestive one is described in de la Primaudaye's *Académie Française*, translated into English in 1586. The grouping and pairing of characters, as well as several episodes in the play, show the influence of comedies by John Lyly written between 1584 and 1587. The stock characters of Italian *commedia dell' arte* have helped to shape Armado (*capetano*), Moth (*zanni*), Holofernes (*dottore*), Nathaniel (*pantalone* and parasite), and it seems more plausible that this phenomenon would occur fresh upon the visit of Italian troupes to England rather than a decade later. The selection of the character names Navarre, Berowne (de Biron), Longaville, and Dumaine (du Maine or de Mayenne) would have been more feasible in the 'eighties than in the 'nineties, since the actual French owners of these family names became prominent in a war of blood rather than a war of words after 1589 and *personae non gratae* in England after 1593. An actual early Tudor mask of Muscovites with blackamoor torchbearers is described in Holinshed's *Chronicles,* 1587.

In the large number of parts for juvenile actors (four ladies and a boy), in its construction, spirit, and themes, *Love's Labor's Lost* is more suggestive of earlier chorister drama than of the drama of the Lord Chamberlain's Men. It is conceivable that Shakespeare wrote the play for Paul's theatre in 1588–89 and salvaged it as a novelty for his own company in 1596–97, so that it is unnecessary to postulate *abnormal* auspices of coterie production. Of course there is no proof that such is the case, but until current orthodoxy about the original date and auspices of production is more firmly based, this alternative should be kept in mind. What Shakespeare was doing at the age of twenty-four or twenty-five we do not know, and *Love's Labor's Lost* may provide a clue; speculation in this direction would prove at least as profitable as speculation on whether Armado represents Sir Walter Raleigh, Antonio Perez, or the King of Spain.

Whatever the date of the original version, and whether they first appeared in that version or in the revision, the play contains what Granville-Barker called "outcroppings of pure dramatic gold" – the more surprising and delightful for their sporadic appearance: for instance, the sudden deflation of the jesting Princess when Costard puns on her "thickness" – "What's your will, sir? What's your will?"; or Costard's modest pride in his own acting ability and patronage of Nathaniel's – "a marvellous good neighbor, faith, and a very good bowler; but for Alisander – alas, you see how 'tis – a little o'erparted"; or Holofernes' just reproof (without pedantry) of the merciless courtiers – "This is not generous, not gentle, not humble"; or Armado's defense of Hector – "Sweet chucks, beat not the bones of the buried. When he breathed, he was a man" – and his own manly recovery from humiliation. The ending, afterthought though it seems to be, is wonderfully effective – dissolving the play rather than concluding it, with sudden images of suffering and death, with gravity and tenderness. Here appears in full view the Shakespeare who was *not* only playing with words.

The only performances of *Love's Labor's Lost* of which we

have certain knowledge are the court production mentioned on the title page of 1598 and a second court production, before Queen Anne, in 1605, but the late printing of a quarto in 1631 indicates a revival at Blackfriars. For centuries thereafter critics considered it not only Shakespeare's first but his worst play, and actors preferred to ignore it. It has the distinction of being the only Shakespearean play never performed in the Restoration and the eighteenth and early nineteenth centuries. One can understand why: it offered little opportunity for the increasingly egocentric acting of the great Shakespearean stars from Betterton to Kean, or for the increasing pomposity of Shakespearean staging from Kean to Irving. There were a few isolated productions as the nineteenth century progressed, by Madam Vestris (1839), Samuel Phelps (1857), and Augustin Daly (1874–91). Irving dismissed it as impossible, and even Granville-Barker was a little rueful in his commendations. The play has been rescued for the stage by the Shakespeare Festival companies, the Old Vic, and academic and experimental groups. Those who see it performed are delighted, and wonder why they have not had more frequent opportunities.

In a good performance the play even achieves a kind of homogeneity. Just as the final episode mitigates the frivolity which precedes, the closing songs mitigate the solemnity of the final episode. They are the songs of a very relaxed Apollo, so effortless as to seem to have grown like the "daisies pied and violets blue" rather than to have been composed, yet sharply focused upon realities and technically superb. They are nostalgic and gently ribald, like the closing song of *Twelfth Night,* but in some mysterious way they place our world in perspective.

*Harvard University*                    ALFRED HARBAGE

*Note on the text: Love's Labor's Lost* was published in 1598 in a quarto almost certainly printed from the author's manuscript. If there was an earlier quarto, no copies have survived. The folio text was printed from the quarto, probably without independent authority. The text of the quarto contains numerous imperfections, owing in part to persisting confusion in the manuscript and to the compositor's difficulty in following word-play, especially that involving foreign languages. The present edition adheres when possible to the text of the quarto, and all material departures are indicated in an appendix. The act-scene division indicated marginally is that of the Globe text, which follows the divisions of the quarto except that it splits the first act into two scenes.

# Love's Labor's Lost

[Names of the Actors

Ferdinand, *King of Navarre*
Berowne ⎱
Longaville ⎬ *lords attending on the King in his retirement*
Dumaine ⎰
Boyet ⎱ *lords attending on the Princess of France*
Marcade ⎰
Don Adriano de Armado, *a fantastical Spaniard*
Nathaniel, *a curate*
Dull, *a constable*
Holofernes, *a schoolmaster*
Costard, *a clown*
Moth, *page to Don Adriano de Armado*
A Forester
Princess of France
Rosaline ⎱
Maria ⎬ *ladies attending on the Princess*
Katharine ⎰
Jaquenetta, *a country wench*
Officers and other Attendants

Scene
Navarre]

# LOVE'S LABOR'S LOST

*Enter Ferdinand King of Navarre, Berowne, Longaville,*   I, i
*and Dumaine.*

*King.* Let fame, that all hunt after in their lives,
Live regist'red upon our brazen tombs
And then grace us in the disgrace of death;
When, spite of cormorant devouring time,
Th' endeavor of this present breath may buy          5
That honor which shall bate his scythe's keen edge
And make us heirs of all eternity.
Therefore, brave conquerors — for so you are
That war against your own affections
And the huge army of the world's desires —          10
Our late edict shall strongly stand in force:
Navarre shall be the wonder of the world;
Our court shall be a little academe,
Still and contemplative in living art.
You three, Berowne, Dumaine, and Longaville,          15
Have sworn for three years' term to live with me,
My fellow scholars, and to keep those statutes

I, i, 3 *disgrace* deterioration   4 *cormorant* ravenous   5 *breath* breathing-
time   6 *bate* blunt   9 *affections* passions   13 *academe* academy   14 *Still . . .
art* constantly contemplative of the art of living

That are recorded in this schedule here.
Your oaths are passed; and now subscribe your names,
20  That his own hand may strike his honor down
That violates the smallest branch herein.
If you are armed to do as sworn to do,
Subscribe to your deep oaths, and keep it too.
*Longaville.* I am resolved. 'Tis but a three years' fast.
25  The mind shall banquet though the body pine.
Fat paunches have lean pates, and dainty bits
Make rich the ribs, but bankrout quite the wits.
*Dumaine.* My loving lord, Dumaine is mortified.
The grosser manner of these world's delights
30  He throws upon the gross world's baser slaves.
To love, to wealth, to pomp, I pine and die,
With all these living in philosophy.
*Berowne.* I can but say their protestation over;
So much, dear liege, I have already sworn,
35  That is, to live and study here three years.
But there are other strict observances:
As not to see a woman in that term,
Which I hope well is not enrollèd there;
And one day in a week to touch no food,
40  And but one meal on every day beside,
The which I hope is not enrollèd there;
And then to sleep but three hours in the night,
And not be seen to wink of all the day
(When I was wont to think no harm all night
45  And make a dark night too of half the day),
Which I hope well is not enrollèd there.

20 *hand* i.e. testimony of handwriting, signature  21 *branch* subdivision,
by-law  27 *bankrout* bankrupt  28 *mortified* i.e. dead to desire  32 *all
these* i.e. his companions (?) or love, wealth, pomp, of which philosophy
will prove the equivalent (?)  43 *wink* close the eyes, nap  44 *think no
harm* i.e. sleep

O, these are barren tasks, too hard to keep —
Not to see ladies, study, fast, not sleep.
*King.* Your oath is passed to pass away from these.
*Berowne.* Let me say no, my liege, an if you please.          50
    I only swore to study with your Grace
    And stay here in your court for three years' space.
*Longaville.* You swore to that, Berowne, and to the rest.
*Berowne.* By yea and nay, sir, then I swore in jest.
    What is the end of study, let me know?          55
*King.* Why, that to know which else we should not know.
*Berowne.* Things hid and barred, you mean, from common
    sense?
*King.* Ay, that is study's godlike recompense.
*Berowne.* Come on then, I will swear to study so,
    To know the thing I am forbid to know:          60
    As thus — to study where I well may dine
    When I to feast expressly am forbid;
    Or study where to meet some mistress fine
    When mistresses from common sense are hid;
    Or having sworn too hard-a-keeping oath,          65
    Study to break it and not break my troth.
    If study's gain be thus, and this be so,
    Study knows that which yet it doth not know.
    Swear me to this, and I will ne'er say no.
*King.* These be the stops that hinder study quite,          70
    And train our intellects to vain delight.
*Berowne.* Why, all delights are vain, but that most vain
    Which, with pain purchased, doth inherit pain:
    As, painfully to pore upon a book,

50 *an if* if   54 *By . . . nay* (1) irrevocably (derived in popular usage from
Matthew 5:37) (2) equivocally (in Berowne's play on the literal meaning)
57 *common sense* ordinary observation   70 *stops* impediments   71 *train*
allure   73 *inherit* take possession of

31

75 To seek the light of truth, while truth the while
Doth falsely blind the eyesight of his look.
Light seeking light doth light of light beguile;
So, ere you find where light in darkness lies,
Your light grows dark by losing of your eyes.

80 Study me how to please the eye indeed,
By fixing it upon a fairer eye,
Who dazzling so, that eye shall be his heed,
And give him light that it was blinded by.
Study is like the heaven's glorious sun,

85 That will not be deep-searched with saucy looks:
Small have continual plodders ever won,
Save base authority from others' books.
These earthly godfathers of heaven's lights,
That give a name to every fixèd star,

90 Have no more profit of their shining nights
Than those that walk and wot not what they are.
Too much to know is to know nought but fame;
And every godfather can give a name.

*King.* How well he's read to reason against reading!

95 *Dumaine.* Proceeded well, to stop all good proceeding!

*Longaville.* He weeds the corn, and still lets grow the
weeding.

*Berowne.* The spring is near, when green geese are a-breed-
ing.

*Dumaine.* How follows that?

76 *falsely* treacherously  *his look* its power to see  77 *Light . . . beguile* i.e.
peering for truth deprives the eyes of their sight  79 *light* sight  80 *Study
me* study for me  82 *dazzling so* thus bedazzled  *heed* guide  83 *it* i.e. his
eye  88 *earthly godfathers* i.e. the astronomers  90 *shining* i.e. star-lit  91
*wot* know  92 *know nought* experience nothing  93 *every . . . name* i.e.
anyone who serves as a godfather can do as much as astronomers do
94 *read . . . reading* studied . . . studying  95 *Proceeded* i.e. advanced
through the academic curriculum  96 *weeds the corn* i.e. pulls up the wheat
*weeding* weeds  97 *green geese* young geese, fools

*Berowne.*                     Fit in his place and time.
*Dumaine.* In reason nothing.
*Berowne.*                     Something then in rime.
*King.* Berowne is like an envious sneaping frost          100
  That bites the first-born infants of the spring.
*Berowne.* Well, say I am; why should proud summer boast
  Before the birds have any cause to sing?
  Why should I joy in an abortive birth?
  At Christmas I no more desire a rose                    105
  Than wish a snow in May's new-fangled shows;
  But like of each thing that in season grows.
  So you, to study now it is too late,
  Climb o'er the house to unlock the little gate.
*King.* Well, sit you out. Go home, Berowne. Adieu.       110
*Berowne.* No, my good lord, I have sworn to stay with you;
  And though I have for barbarism spoke more
  Than for that angel knowledge you can say,
  Yet confident I'll keep what I have sworn,
  And bide the penance of each three years' day.          115
  Give me the paper, let me read the same,
  And to the strictest decrees I'll write my name.
*King.* How well this yielding rescues thee from shame!
*Berowne.* [*reads*] 'Item. That no woman shall come within a
  mile of my court —' Hath this been proclaimed?          120
*Longaville.* Four days ago.
*Berowne.* Let's see the penalty. ' — on pain of losing her
  tongue.' Who devised this penalty?
*Longaville.* Marry, that did I.

98 *Fit in his* precisely in its  100 *sneaping* nipping  101 *first-born infants*
i.e. early buds  102–3 *why . . . sing* i.e. why should summer appear un-
seasonably  108 *too late* i.e. past his student days  109 *Climb . . . gate* i.e.
act perversely (proverbial)  112 *barbarism* primitive ignorance  115 *bide
. . . day* i.e. endure the deprivation each day of the three years  124 *Marry*
by Mary (mild oath)

*Berowne.*                              Sweet lord, and why?

125 *Longaville.* To fright them hence with that dread penalty.

*Berowne.* A dangerous law against gentility!

   *[Reads]* 'Item. If any man be seen to talk with a woman
   within the term of three years, he shall endure such public
   shame as the rest of the court can possibly devise.'

130 This article, my liege, yourself must break;
   For well you know here comes in embassy
   The French king's daughter with yourself to speak,
   A maid of grace and complete majesty,
   About surrender up of Aquitaine

135 To her decrepit, sick, and bed-rid father.
   Therefore this article is made in vain,
   Or vainly comes th' admirèd princess hither.

*King.* What say you, lords? why, this was quite forgot.

*Berowne.* So study evermore is overshot.

140 While it doth study to have what it would,
   It doth forget to do the thing it should;
   And when it hath the thing it hunteth most,
   'Tis won as towns with fire; so won, so lost.

*King.* We must of force dispense with this decree;

145 She must lie here on mere necessity.

*Berowne.* Necessity will make us all forsworn
   Three thousand times within this three years' space:
   For every man with his affects is born,
   Not by might mast'red, but by special grace.

150 If I break faith, this word shall speak for me,
   I am forsworn 'on mere necessity.'
   So to the laws at large I write my name;        *[Signs.]*
   And he that breaks them in the least degree

---

126 *gentility* civilized custom  143 *as . . . fire* i.e. like towns conquered by
being burned down  144 *of force* perforce  145 *lie* lodge  148 *affects* passions  149 *might* i.e. his own strength  *special grace* heavenly intervention

Stands in attainder of eternal shame.
Suggestions are to other as to me;                                    155
But I believe, although I seem so loath,
I am the last that will last keep his oath.
But is there no quick recreation granted?
*King.* Ay, that there is. Our court you know is haunted
  With a refinèd traveller of Spain,                          160
  A man in all the world's new fashion planted,
  That hath a mint of phrases in his brain;
  One who the music of his own vain tongue
  Doth ravish like enchanting harmony;
  A man of complements, whom right and wrong          165
  Have chose as umpire of their mutiny.
  This child of fancy, that Armado hight,
  For interim to our studies shall relate
  In high-born words the worth of many a knight
  From tawny Spain, lost in the world's debate.       170
  How you delight, my lords, I know not, I;
  But, I protest, I love to hear him lie,
  And I will use him for my minstrelsy.
*Berowne.* Armado is a most illustrious wight,
  A man of fire-new words, fashion's own knight.      175
*Longaville.* Costard the swain and he shall be our sport;
  And so to study three years is but short.

*Enter [Dull,] a Constable, with Costard, with a letter.*

*Constable.* Which is the duke's own person?
*Berowne.* This, fellow. What wouldst?

154 *in attainder* under penalty   155 *Suggestions* temptations   158 *quick*
lively   159–60 *haunted With* visited by   160 *refinèd* precious   161 *planted*
rooted   165 *complements* affectations   166 *umpire . . . mutiny* i.e. rational-
izer   167 *hight* is called   168 *interim* recess   169 *high-born* i.e. highfalutin
170 *tawny* sunburnt   *debate* warfare   173 *minstrelsy* i.e. diversion   175 *fire-
new* brand-new   176 *swain* country youth

180 *Constable.* I myself reprehend his own person, for I am his
Grace's farborough; but I would see his own person in
flesh and blood.

*Berowne.* This is he.

*Constable.* Signior Arm — Arm — commends you. There's
185 villainy abroad. This letter will tell you more.

*Costard.* Sir, the contempts thereof are as touching me.

*King.* A letter from the magnificent Armado.

*Berowne.* How low soever the matter, I hope in God for
high words.

190 *Longaville.* A high hope for a low heaven. God grant us patience!

*Berowne.* To hear, or forbear hearing?

*Longaville.* To hear meekly, sir, and to laugh moderately, or
to forbear both.

195 *Berowne.* Well, sir, be it as the style shall give us cause to
climb in the merriness.

*Costard.* The matter is to me, sir, as concerning Jaquenetta.
The manner of it is, I was taken with the manner.

*Berowne.* In what manner?

200 *Costard.* In manner and form following, sir; all those three:
I was seen with her in the manor-house, sitting with her
upon the form, and taken following her into the park;
which, put together, is, in manner and form following.
Now, sir, for the manner — it is the manner of a man to
205 speak to a woman. For the form — in some form.

*Berowne.* For the following, sir?

---

180 *reprehend* i.e. represent (malapropism)   181 *farborough* petty constable   186 *contempts* i.e. contents (malapropism)   187 *magnificent Armado*
(play on magnificent or 'grand' Armada)   190 *low heaven* i.e. small bless-
ing   192 *To hear . . . hearing* i.e. to take it or leave it   195 *be it* so be it
197 *is to* applies to   198 *with the manner* in the act (from legal term
'mainour')   202 *form* bench

*Costard.* As it shall follow in my correction, and God defend
the right!

*King.* Will you hear this letter with attention?

*Berowne.* As we would hear an oracle.                    210

*Costard.* Such is the simplicity of man to hearken after the
flesh.

*King. [reads]* 'Great deputy, the welkin's vicegerent, and
sole dominator of Navarre, my soul's earth's God, and
body's fostering patron —'                    215

*Costard.* Not a word of Costard yet.

*King.* 'So it is —'

*Costard.* It may be so; but if he say it is so, he is, in telling
true, but so.

*King.* Peace!                    220

*Costard.* Be to me and every man that dares not fight.

*King.* No words!

*Costard.* Of other men's secrets, I beseech you.

*King.* 'So it is, besieged with sable-colored melancholy, I
did commend the black-oppressing humor to the most    225
wholesome physic of thy health-giving air; and, as I am a
gentleman, betook myself to walk. The time when?
About the sixth hour; when beasts most graze, birds best
peck, and men sit down to that nourishment which is
called supper: so much for the time when. Now for the    230
ground which; which, I mean, I walked upon: it is
ycleped thy park. Then for the place where; where, I
mean, I did encounter that obscene and most preposterous
event, that draweth from my snow-white pen the ebon-
colored ink, which here thou viewest, beholdest, survey-    235
est, or seest. But to the place where, it standeth north-

---

207 *correction* punishment   213 *welkin's vicegerent* heaven's deputy   219
*but so* only in part   226 *physic* cure   232 *ycleped* called

north-east and by east from the west corner of thy curious-knotted garden. There did I see that low-spirited
swain, that base minnow of thy mirth —'
240 *Costard.* Me?
*King.* 'that unlettered small-knowing soul —'
*Costard.* Me?
*King.* 'that shallow vessel —'
*Costard.* Still me.
245 *King.* 'which, as I remember, hight Costard —'
*Costard.* O me!
*King.* 'sorted and consorted, contrary to thy established
proclaimed edict and continent canon, which with — O,
with — but with this I passion to say wherewith —'
250 *Costard.* With a wench.
*King.* 'with a child of our grandmother Eve, a female; or,
for thy more sweet understanding, a woman. Him I (as
my ever-esteemed duty pricks me on) have sent to thee,
to receive the meed of punishment, by thy sweet Grace's
255 officer, Anthony Dull, a man of good repute, carriage,
bearing, and estimation.'
*Dull.* Me, an't shall please you; I am Anthony Dull.
*King.* 'For Jaquenetta (so is the weaker vessel called), which
I apprehended with the aforesaid swain, I keep her as a
260 vessel of thy law's fury; and shall, at the least of thy sweet
notice, bring her to trial. Thine in all compliments of
devoted and heart-burning heat of duty,
                    Don Adriano de Armado.'
*Berowne.* This is not so well as I looked for, but the best
265 that ever I heard.

237–38 *curious-knotted* intricately patterned  239 *minnow* i.e. small-fry
245 *hight* is called  247 *sorted* associated  248 *continent canon* law enjoining
celibacy  249 *passion* grieve  253 *pricks* spurs  260–61 *at . . . notice* i.e. at
your first hint

*King.* Ay, the best for the worst. But, sirrah, what say you
    to this?

*Costard.* Sir, I confess the wench.

*King.* Did you hear the proclamation?

*Costard.* I do confess much of the hearing it, but little of the   270
    marking of it.

*King.* It was proclaimed a year's imprisonment to be taken
    with a wench.

*Costard.* I was taken with none, sir; I was taken with a
    damsel.   275

*King.* Well, it was proclaimed 'damsel.'

*Costard.* This was no damsel neither, sir; she was a virgin.

*King.* It is so varied too, for it was proclaimed 'virgin.'

*Costard.* If it were, I deny her virginity; I was taken with a
    maid.   280

*King.* This maid will not serve your turn, sir.

*Costard.* This maid will serve my turn, sir.

*King.* Sir, I will pronounce your sentence: you shall fast a
    week with bran and water.

*Costard.* I had rather pray a month with mutton and por-   285
    ridge.

*King.* And Don Armado shall be your keeper.
    My Lord Berowne, see him delivered o'er:
    And go we, lords, to put in practice that
    Which each to other hath so strongly sworn.   290
            *[Exeunt King, Longaville, and Dumaine.]*

*Berowne.* I'll lay my head to any good man's hat,
    These oaths and laws will prove an idle scorn.
    Sirrah, come on.

266 *best . . . worst* i.e. prize example of the bad   *sirrah* (contemptuous or
admonitory term of address)   278 *varied* (synonyms in the legal fashion
were used in the proclamation)   281 *turn* purpose (with ribald pun following)   285–86 *mutton and porridge* mutton-broth

*Costard.* I suffer for the truth, sir; for true it is I was taken
295    with Jaquenetta, and Jaquenetta is a true girl; and therefore welcome the sour cup of prosperity! Affliction may
one day smile again, and till then sit thee down, sorrow!

                                  *Exeunt.*

**I, ii**       *Enter Armado, [a Braggart,] and Moth, his Page.*

*Armado.* Boy, what sign is it when a man of great spirit
grows melancholy?

*Moth.* A great sign, sir, that he will look sad.

*Armado.* Why, sadness is one and the selfsame thing, dear
5    imp.

*Moth.* No, no. O Lord, sir, no!

*Armado.* How canst thou part sadness and melancholy, my
tender juvenal?

*Moth.* By a familiar demonstration of the working, my
10    tough signor.

*Armado.* Why tough signor? why tough signor?

*Moth.* Why tender juvenal? why tender juvenal?

*Armado.* I spoke it, tender juvenal, as a congruent epitheton
appertaining to thy young days, which we may nominate
15    tender.

*Moth.* And I, tough signor, as an appertinent title to your
old time, which we may name tough.

---

296 *prosperity! Affliction* (malapropisms)   297 *sit thee down* i.e. abide with
me   I, ii, 5 *imp* young shoot, child   7 *part* distinguish between   8 *juvenal*
youth   9 *working* operation   10 *signor* sir (with pun on senior)   13 *congruent epitheton* appropriate epithet   16 *appertinent* belonging

*Armado.* Pretty, and apt.

*Moth.* How mean you, sir? I pretty, and my saying apt? or
I apt, and my saying pretty?                                    20

*Armado.* Thou pretty, because little.

*Moth.* Little pretty, because little. Wherefore apt?

*Armado.* And therefore apt, because quick.

*Moth.* Speak you this in my praise, master?

*Armado.* In thy condign praise.                               25

*Moth.* I will praise an eel with the same praise.

*Armado.* What, that an eel is ingenious?

*Moth.* That an eel is quick.

*Armado.* I do say thou art quick in answers. Thou heat'st
my blood.                                                      30

*Moth.* I am answered, sir.

*Armado.* I love not to be crossed.

*Moth. [aside]* He speaks the mere contrary – crosses love
not him.

*Armado.* I have promised to study three years with the duke. 35

*Moth.* You may do it in an hour, sir.

*Armado.* Impossible.

*Moth.* How many is one thrice told?

*Armado.* I am ill at reckoning; it fitteth the spirit of a tap-
ster.                                                          40

*Moth.* You are a gentleman and a gamester, sir.

*Armado.* I confess both. They are both the varnish of a complete man.

*Moth.* Then, I am sure you know how much the gross sum
of deuce-ace amounts to.                                       45

*Armado.* It doth amount to one more than two.

---

25 *condign* well-merited   28 *quick* quick-bodied (whereas Armado had
used the word to mean quick-witted or ingenious)   29–30 *heat'st my blood*
anger me   33 *crosses* coins (which were commonly stamped with crosses)
35 *duke* i.e. the ruler, actually a king   42 *varnish* ornament, finish

*Moth.* Which the base vulgar do call three.

*Armado.* True.

*Moth.* Why, sir, is this such a piece of study? Now here is
50    three studied ere ye'll thrice wink; and how easy it is to
put 'years' to the word 'three,' and study three years in
two words, the dancing horse will tell you.

*Armado.* A most fine figure.

*Moth. [aside]* To prove you a cipher.

55 *Armado.* I will hereupon confess I am in love; and as it is
base for a soldier to love, so am I in love with a base
wench. If drawing my sword against the humor of affection would deliver me from the reprobate thought of
it, I would take Desire prisoner and ransom him to any
60    French courtier for a new devised curtsy. I think scorn to
sigh: methinks I should outswear Cupid. Comfort me,
boy. What great men have been in love?

*Moth.* Hercules, master.

*Armado.* Most sweet Hercules! More authority, dear boy,
65    name more; and, sweet my child, let them be men of
good repute and carriage.

*Moth.* Samson, master — he was a man of good carriage,
great carriage, for he carried the town-gates on his back
like a porter, and he was in love.

70 *Armado.* O well-knit Samson! strong-jointed Samson! I do
excel thee in my rapier as much as thou didst me in carry-
ing gates. I am in love too. Who was Samson's love, my
dear Moth?

*Moth.* A woman, master.

47 *vulgar* common people   52 *dancing horse* (a performing horse, trained to
'count' in hoof-beats; the most famous of the time was Master Banks'
horse Morocco)   53 *figure* metaphor (with play on numeral)   57–58
*humor of affection* inclination to passion   60 *new devised curtsy* i.e. new-
fangled French bow (abundant and worthless)   *think scorn* disdain   61 *outswear* forswear   66 *carriage* bearing   68 *carried . . . back* (cf. Judges 16:3)

*Armado.* Of what complexion?                              75

*Moth.* Of all the four, or the three, or the two, or one of the
    four.

*Armado.* Tell me precisely of what complexion.

*Moth.* Of the sea-water green, sir.

*Armado.* Is that one of the four complexions?            80

*Moth.* As I have read, sir, and the best of them too.

*Armado.* Green indeed is the color of lovers; but to have a
    love of that color, methinks Samson had small reason for
    it. He surely affected her for her wit.

*Moth.* It was so, sir, for she had a green wit.          85

*Armado.* My love is most immaculate white and red.

*Moth.* Most maculate thoughts, master, are masked under
    such colors.

*Armado.* Define, define, well-educated infant.

*Moth.* My father's wit, and my mother's tongue, assist me!  90

*Armado.* Sweet invocation of a child, most pretty and
    pathetical.

*Moth.* If she be made of white and red,
            Her faults will ne'er be known,
        For blushing cheeks by faults are bred,       95
            And fears by pale white shown;
        Then if she fear, or be to blame,
            By this you shall not know,
        For still her cheeks possess the same
            Which native she doth owe.                 100

75 *complexion* (1) skin-coloring (2) disposition (deriving from the bal-
ance or imbalance of the four bodily 'humors'—blood, choler, phlegm,
melancholy) 76–77 *Of . . . four* (probably an allusion to woman's change-
ableness) 82 *Green . . . lovers* i.e. lovers are prone to 'green-sickness' (the
melancholy of frustration; cf. *Twelfth Night*, II, iv, 116) 82–83 *have a
love of* i.e. love 84 *affected . . . wit* liked her for her intelligence 85 *green
wit* (1) immature mind (2) a play on the 'green withes' with which De-
lilah bound Samson (cf. Judges 16:7–9) 92 *pathetical* moving 100 *native*
naturally, by birth *owe* own

A dangerous rime, master, against the reason of white and
red.

*Armado.* Is there not a ballet, boy, of the King and the
Beggar?

105 *Moth.* The world was very guilty of such a ballet some three
ages since; but I think now 'tis not to be found; or if it
were, it would neither serve for the writing nor the tune.

*Armado.* I will have that subject newly writ o'er, that I may
example my digression by some mighty precedent. Boy,
110 I do love that country girl that I took in the park with the
rational hind Costard. She deserves well.

*Moth.* [*aside*] To be whipped; and yet a better love than my
master.

*Armado.* Sing, boy. My spirit grows heavy in love.

115 *Moth.* And that's great marvel, loving a light wench.

*Armado.* I say, sing.

*Moth.* Forbear till this company be past.

*Enter [Costard, the] Clown, [Dull, the] Constable, and
[Jaquenetta, a] Wench.*

*Dull.* Sir, the duke's pleasure is, that you keep Costard safe,
and you must suffer him to take no delight nor no pen-
120 ance, but 'a must fast three days a week. For this damsel,
I must keep her at the park; she is allowed for the day-
woman. Fare you well.

*Armado.* I do betray myself with blushing. Maid!

*Jaquenetta.* Man?

101 *the reason of* the case for   103 *ballet* ballad   103–4 *King . . . Beggar* (the
ballad of King Cophetua, who fell in love with a beggar-maid; cf. IV, i,
65–67)   107 *serve* be adequate   109 *example* justify   *digression* deviation,
lapse   111 *rational* i.e. rational for a yokel (patronizing rather than compli-
mentary)   112 *love* partner in a love-affair   119–20 *penance* (a malapropism, possibly for 'pleasaunce')   120 *'a* he   121–22 *allowed . . . day-woman*
approved as the dairy-maid

*Armado.* I will visit thee at the lodge.                    125
*Jaquenetta.* That's hereby.
*Armado.* I know where it is situate.
*Jaquenetta.* Lord, how wise you are!
*Armado.* I will tell thee wonders.
*Jaquenetta.* With that face?                    130
*Armado.* I love thee.
*Jaquenetta.* So I heard you say.
*Armado.* And so farewell.
*Jaquenetta.* Fair weather after you!
*Dull.* Come, Jaquenetta, away!                    135

*Exeunt [Dull and Jaquenetta].*

*Armado.* Villain, thou shalt fast for thy offenses ere thou be
   pardoned.
*Costard.* Well, sir, I hope when I do it I shall do it on a full
   stomach.
*Armado.* Thou shalt be heavily punished.                    140
*Costard.* I am more bound to you than your fellows, for
   they are but lightly rewarded.
*Armado.* Take away this villain. Shut him up.
*Moth.* Come, you transgressing slave, away!
*Costard.* Let me not be pent up, sir. I will fast, being loose.    145
*Moth.* No, sir; that were fast and loose. Thou shalt to
   prison.
*Costard.* Well, if ever I do see the merry days of desolation
   that I have seen, some shall see —
*Moth.* What shall some see?                    150
*Costard.* Nay, nothing, Master Moth, but what they look
   upon. It is not for prisoners to be too silent in their words,

130 *With that face* i.e. you don't say so (slang; all of Jaquenetta's smart
replies seem to be rustic cant)   138–39 *on . . . stomach* (1) courageously (2)
well-fed   146 *fast and loose* cheating (deriving from a game involving
cheating and associated with gypsies)   148 *desolation* (malapropism, possibly for 'consolation')

and therefore I will say nothing. I thank God I have as
little patience as another man, and therefore I can be quiet.

*Exit [with Moth].*

155 *Armado.* I do affect the very ground (which is base) where
her shoe (which is baser) guided by her foot (which is
basest) doth tread. I shall be forsworn (which is a great argument of falsehood) if I love. And how can that be true
love which is falsely attempted? Love is a familiar; Love
160 is a devil. There is no evil angel but Love. Yet was Samson so tempted, and he had an excellent strength; yet was
Solomon so seduced, and he had a very good wit. Cupid's
butt-shaft is too hard for Hercules' club, and therefore too
much odds for a Spaniard's rapier. The first and second
165 cause will not serve my turn: the passado he respects not,
the duello he regards not. His disgrace is to be called boy,
but his glory is to subdue men. Adieu, valor! rust, rapier!
be still, drum! for your manager is in love; yea, he
loveth. Assist me some extemporal god of rime, for I am
170 sure I shall turn sonnet. Devise, wit! write, pen! for I am
for whole volumes in folio.                          *Exit.*

---

155 *affect* love  157-58 *argument* proof  159 *familiar* evil spirit  163 *butt-
shaft* unbarbed target arrow  164-65 *first . . . cause* (an allusion to certain
procedures dictated by the punctilio of the duelling code)  165 *passado*
fencing thrust  166 *duello* duelling code  168 *manager* skilled manipulator
169 *extemporal . . . rime* god of fluent occasional verses  170 *turn sonnet*
compose a sonnet (?) turn sonneteer (?)

*Enter the Princess of France, with three attending Ladies,* II, i
*[Rosaline, Maria, Katharine,] and three Lords, [one of*
*whom is Boyet].*

*Boyet.* Now, madam, summon up your dearest spirits.
Consider who the king your father sends,
To whom he sends, and what's his embassy:
Yourself, held precious in the world's esteem,
To parley with the sole inheritor                          5
Of all perfections that a man may owe,
Matchless Navarre; the plea of no less weight
Than Aquitaine, a dowry for a queen.
Be now as prodigal of all dear grace
As Nature was in making graces dear,                       10
When she did starve the general world beside,
And prodigally gave them all to you.
*Princess.* Good Lord Boyet, my beauty, though but mean,
Needs not the painted flourish of your praise:
Beauty is bought by judgment of the eye,                   15
Not uttered by base sale of chapmen's tongues.
I am less proud to hear you tell my worth
Than you much willing to be counted wise
In spending your wit in the praise of mine.
But now to task the tasker: good Boyet,                    20
You are not ignorant, all-telling fame
Doth noise abroad, Navarre hath made a vow,
Till painful study shall outwear three years,
No woman may approach his silent court:
Therefore to's seemeth it a needful course,                25

II, i, 1 *dearest spirits* best wits   3 *what's* the nature of   5 *inheritor* possessor
6 *owe* own   7 *plea* suit   14 *flourish* adornment   16 *uttered* vended   *chap-*
*men's* retailers'   17 *tell* speak of (with play on count)   20 *task* assign tasks
to   23 *painful* strenuous   *outwear* last out   25 *to's* to us (royal plural)

47

Before we enter his forbidden gates,
To know his pleasure; and in that behalf,
Bold of your worthiness, we single you
As our best-moving fair solicitor.

30    Tell him, the daughter of the King of France,
On serious business, craving quick dispatch,
Importunes personal conference with his Grace.
Haste, signify so much; while we attend,
Like humble-visaged suitors, his high will.

35  *Boyet.* Proud of employment, willingly I go.          *Exit Boyet.*
*Princess.* All pride is willing pride, and yours is so.
Who are the votaries, my loving lords,
That are vow-fellows with this virtuous duke?
*Lord.* Longaville is one.
*Princess.*                           Know you the man?

40  *Maria.* I know him, madam. At a marriage feast
Between Lord Perigort and the beauteous heir
Of Jacques Falconbridge solemnizèd
In Normandy saw I this Longaville.
A man of sovereign parts he is esteemed,

45    Well fitted in arts, glorious in arms;
Nothing becomes him ill that he would well.
The only soil of his fair virtue's gloss
(If virtue's gloss will stain with any soil)
Is a sharp wit matched with too blunt a will,

50    Whose edge hath power to cut, whose will still wills

---

28 *Bold* confident   29 *best-moving fair* most persuasive and just   36 *All
. . . pride* i.e. all pride derives from man's rebellious will (?)   37 *votaries*
those living under a vow, often including a vow of celibacy   41–42 *Lord
Perigort, Jacques Falconbridge* (fictitious persons)   45 *fitted in arts* equipped
with learning   46 *Nothing . . . well* i.e. lacking in no grace he values   47
*soil of* blot on   49 *blunt* ruthless   50 *Whose edge* i.e. the edge of his sharp
wit

It should none spare that come within his power.
*Princess.* Some merry mocking lord, belike – is 't so?
*Maria.* They say so most that most his humors know.
*Princess.* Such short-lived wits do wither as they grow.
　　Who are the rest?                                                    55
*Katharine.* The young Dumaine, a well-accomplished
　　youth,
　　Of all that virtue love for virtue loved;
　　Most power to do most harm, least knowing ill,
　　For he hath wit to make an ill shape good,
　　And shape to win grace though he had no wit.               60
　　I saw him at the Duke Alençon's once;
　　And much too little of that good I saw
　　Is my report to his great worthiness.
*Rosaline.* Another of these students at that time
　　Was there with him, if I have heard a truth.               65
　　Berowne they call him; but a merrier man,
　　Within the limit of becoming mirth,
　　I never spent an hour's talk withal.
　　His eye begets occasion for his wit;
　　For every object that the one doth catch                ·      70
　　The other turns to a mirth-moving jest,
　　Which his fair tongue, conceit's expositor,
　　Delivers in such apt and gracious words,
　　That agèd ears play truant at his tales,
　　And younger hearings are quite ravishèd,                    75
　　So sweet and voluble is his discourse.

57 *Of . . . loved* loved for his virtue by all who love virtue   58–60 *Most
. . . wit* (the sense seems to be that the most virtuous people, like Dumaine,
can do the most harm, because they induce in us a fallacious *belief* in per-
fection; in them even vices look like virtues)   62 *little* short   63 *to* compared with, in view of   68 *withal* with   72 *conceit's* fancy's   74 *play
truant* i.e. neglect serious matters   76 *voluble* fluent

*Princess.* God bless my ladies! Are they all in love,
That every one her own hath garnishèd
With such bedecking ornaments of praise?
*Lord.* Here comes Boyet.

*Enter Boyet.*

80  *Princess.*                    Now, what admittance, lord?
*Boyet.* Navarre had notice of your fair approach;
And he and his competitors in oath
Were all addressed to meet you, gentle lady,
Before I came. Marry, thus much I have learnt;
85  He rather means to lodge you in the field,
Like one that comes here to besiege his court,
Than seek a dispensation for his oath
To let you enter his unpeopled house.

*Enter Navarre, Longaville, Dumaine, and Berowne.*

Here comes Navarre.
90  *King.* Fair princess, welcome to the court of Navarre.
*Princess.* 'Fair' I give you back again; and 'welcome' I have
not yet. The roof of this court is too high to be yours, and
welcome to the wide fields too base to be mine.
*King.* You shall be welcome, madam, to my court.
95  *Princess.* I will be welcome, then. Conduct me thither.
*King.* Hear me, dear lady — I have sworn an oath.
*Princess.* Our Lady help my lord! he'll be forsworn.
*King.* Not for the world, fair madam, by my will.
*Princess.* Why, will shall break it; will, and nothing else.
100  *King.* Your ladyship is ignorant what it is.
*Princess.* Were my lord so, his ignorance were wise,

82 *competitors* partners  83 *addressed* prepared  88 *unpeopled* without serv-
ants  92 *roof . . . court* i.e. the heavens  98 *by my will* willingly

Where now his knowledge must prove ignorance.
I hear your Grace hath sworn out house-keeping:
'Tis deadly sin to keep that oath, my lord,
And sin to break it.                                               105
But pardon me, I am too sudden-bold:
To teach a teacher ill beseemeth me.
Vouchsafe to read the purpose of my coming,
And suddenly resolve me in my suit.    *[Gives a paper.]*
*King.* Madam, I will, if suddenly I may.                         110
*Princess.* You will the sooner that I were away,
    For you'll prove perjured if you make me stay.
*Berowne.* Did not I dance with you in Brabant once?
*Rosaline.* Did not I dance with you in Brabant once?
*Berowne.* I know you did.
*Rosaline.*                    How needless was it then           115
    To ask the question!
*Berowne.*              You must not be so quick.
*Rosaline.* 'Tis 'long of you that spur me with such questions.
*Berowne.* Your wit's too hot, it speeds too fast, 'twill tire.
*Rosaline.* Not till it leave the rider in the mire.
*Berowne.* What time o' day?                                      120
*Rosaline.* The hour that fools should ask.
*Berowne.* Now fair befall your mask!
*Rosaline.* Fair fall the face it covers!
*Berowne.* And send you many lovers!
*Rosaline.* Amen, so you be none.                                 125
*Berowne.* Nay, then will I be gone.
*King.* Madam, your father here doth intimate
    The payment of a hundred thousand crowns;

---

102 *Where* whereas   103 *sworn out house-keeping* sworn away hospitality
109 *suddenly resolve* quickly dispatch   111 *that . . . away* to procure my
absence   117 *'long* because   122 *fair befall* good luck to   123 *fall* befall
127 *doth intimate* goes into, canvasses

Being but the one half of an entire sum
130    Disbursèd by my father in his wars.
But say that he, or we (as neither have),
Received that sum, yet there remains unpaid
A hundred thousand more; in surety of the which,
One part of Aquitaine is bound to us,
135    Although not valued to the money's worth.
If then the king your father will restore
But that one half which is unsatisfied,
We will give up our right in Aquitaine,
And hold fair friendship with his Majesty.
140    But that, it seems, he little purposeth,
For here he doth demand to have repaid
A hundred thousand crowns; and not demands,
On payment of a hundred thousand crowns,
To have his title live in Aquitaine;
145    Which we much rather had depart withal,
And have the money by our father lent,
Than Aquitaine, so gelded as it is.
Dear princess, were not his requests so far
From reason's yielding, your fair self should make
150    A yielding 'gainst some reason in my breast,
And go well satisfied to France again.
*Princess.* You do the king my father too much wrong,
And wrong the reputation of your name,
In so unseeming to confess receipt
155    Of that which hath so faithfully been paid.
*King.* I do protest I never heard of it;

---

135 *valued* equal in value   142 *and not demands* i.e. instead of demanding
147 *gelded* maimed, stripped   150 *A . . . reason* i.e. a fairly reasonable yielding (as compared with the totally unreasonable one proposed by her
father)   154 *unseeming* not seeming

And if you prove it, I'll repay it back
Or yield up Aquitaine.
*Princess.* We arrest your word.
Boyet, you can produce acquittances
For such a sum from special officers 160
Of Charles his father.
*King.* Satisfy me so.
*Boyet.* So please your Grace, the packet is not come
Where that and other specialties are bound.
To-morrow you shall have a sight of them.
*King.* It shall suffice me — at which interview 165
All liberal reason I will yield unto.
Meantime, receive such welcome at my hand
As honor, without breach of honor, may
Make tender of to thy true worthiness.
You may not come, fair princess, within my gates; 170
But here without you shall be so received
As you shall deem yourself lodged in my heart,
Though so denied fair harbor in my house.
Your own good thoughts excuse me, and farewell.
To-morrow shall we visit you again. 175
*Princess.* Sweet health and fair desires consort your Grace.
*King.* Thy own wish wish I thee in every place.
*Exit [with Longaville and Dumaine].*
*Berowne.* Lady, I will commend you to mine own heart.
*Rosaline.* Pray you, do my commendations; I would be
glad to see it. 180
*Berowne.* I would you heard it groan.
*Rosaline.* Is the fool sick?

158 *arrest* seize as hostage   163 *specialties* documentary evidence   169
*tender* offer   172 *As* that   176 *consort* dwell with   182 *fool* (a common
term of affection or humorous abuse)

    *Berowne.* Sick at the heart.
    *Rosaline.* Alack, let it blood.
185 *Berowne.* Would that do it good?
    *Rosaline.* My physic says 'ay.'
    *Berowne.* Will you prick 't with your eye?
    *Rosaline.* No point, with my knife.
    *Berowne.* Now, God save thy life.
190 *Rosaline.* And yours from long living.
    *Berowne.* I cannot stay thanksgiving.         *Exit.*

*Enter Dumaine.*

    *Dumaine.* Sir, I pray you a word: what lady is that same?
    *Boyet.* The heir of Alençon, Katharine her name.
    *Dumaine.* A gallant lady. Monsieur, fare you well.    *Exit.*

*[Enter Longaville.]*

195 *Longaville.* I beseech you a word: what is she in the white?
    *Boyet.* A woman sometimes, an you saw her in the light.
    *Longaville.* Perchance light in the light. I desire her name.
    *Boyet.* She hath but one for herself; to desire that were a
        shame.
    *Longaville.* Pray you, sir, whose daughter?
200 *Boyet.* Her mother's, I have heard.
    *Longaville.* God's blessing on your beard!
    *Boyet.* Good sir, be not offended.
    She is an heir of Falconbridge.
    *Longaville.* Nay, my choler is ended.
205    She is a most sweet lady.
    *Boyet.* Not unlike, sir; that may be.     *Exit Longaville.*

---

184 *let it blood* i.e. cure it by bleeding   188 *No point* no (adapted from
French negative 'ne . . . point' with a pun on 'point')   196 *an* if   197 *light
. . . light* i.e. wanton, if clearly seen

*Enter Berowne.*

*Berowne.* What's her name, in the cap?

*Boyet.* Rosaline, by good hap.

*Berowne.* Is she wedded or no?

*Boyet.* To her will, sir, or so.                                   210

*Berowne.* You are welcome, sir. Adieu.

*Boyet.* Farewell to me, sir, and welcome to you.

                                        *Exit Berowne.*

*Maria.* That last is Berowne, the merry madcap lord.

  Not a word with him but a jest.

*Boyet.*                            And every jest but a word.

*Princess.* It was well done of you to take him at his word. 215

*Boyet.* I was as willing to grapple, as he was to board.

*Katharine.* Two hot sheeps, marry!

*Boyet.*                            And wherefore not ships?

  No sheep, sweet lamb, unless we feed on your lips.

*Katharine.* You sheep, and I pasture: shall that finish the jest?

*Boyet.* So you grant pasture for me.

*Katharine.*                          Not so, gentle beast.        220

  My lips are no common, though several they be.

*Boyet.* Belonging to whom?

*Katharine.*                          To my fortunes and me.

*Princess.* Good wits will be jangling; but, gentles, agree.

  This civil war of wits were much better used

  On Navarre and his book-men, for here 'tis abused.           225

*Boyet.* If my observation (which very seldom lies)

  By the heart's still rhetoric disclosèd with eyes

  Deceive me not now, Navarre is infected.

212 *Farewell . . . you* i.e. I welcome your farewell  215 *take . . . word* i.e.
contend with him at word-play  219 *pasture* (a play on 'pastor,' meaning
shepherd)  221 *common* common grazing ground  *though* since  *several*
two lips (with play on 'several' in the legal sense of private lands as opposed
to common lands)  225 *abused* misused  227 *rhetoric* language

*Princess.* With what?

230 *Boyet.* With that which we lovers entitle affected.

*Princess.* Your reason.

*Boyet.* Why, all his behaviors did make their retire
    To the court of his eye, peeping thorough desire.
    His heart, like an agate, with your print impressèd,
235     Proud with his form, in his eye pride expressèd.
    His tongue, all impatient to speak and not see,
    Did stumble with haste in his eyesight to be;
    All senses to that sense did make their repair,
    To feel only looking on fairest of fair.
240     Methought all his senses were locked in his eye,
    As jewels in crystal for some prince to buy;
    Who, tend'ring their own worth from where they were
        glassed,
    Did point you to buy them, along as you passed.
    His face's own margent did quote such amazes,
245     That all eyes saw his eyes enchanted with gazes.
    I'll give you Aquitaine, and all that is his,
    An you give him for my sake but one loving kiss.

*Princess.* Come to our pavilion. Boyet is disposed.

*Boyet.* But to speak that in words which his eye hath dis-
    closed.

---

230 *affected* being moved by passion   232 *behaviors* attitudes   234 *agate* (initials and designs were commonly engraved—'impressed'—on agates) 235 *with his* with its   *pride* i.e. the eye was proud of the privilege of holding your image   236 *all . . . see* i.e. impatient at being a speaking rather than a seeing organ   237 *in . . . be* i.e. to share the sight of the eyes   239 *To feel only* i.e. to concentrate on   242 *Who, tend'ring* which, offering   *glassed* encased in the crystal of his eyes   243 *point* indicate, invite   244 *His . . . amazes* i.e. his amazed expression was a commentary on what his eyes beheld (commentaries or glosses were often printed on the margins— 'margents'—of books)   246 *I'll give you* i.e. you can have   247 *An* if   248 *disposed* i.e. in the mood

I only have made a mouth of his eye,                    250
    By adding a tongue which I know will not lie.
*Rosaline.* Thou art an old love-monger, and speakest skil-
    fully.
*Maria.* He is Cupid's grandfather, and learns news of him.
*Katharine.* Then was Venus like her mother, for her father
    is but grim.
*Boyet.* Do you hear, my mad wenches?
*Rosaline.*                    No.
*Boyet.*                    What, then, do you see? 255
*Rosaline.* Ay, our way to be gone.
*Boyet.*                    You are too hard for me.
                    *Exeunt omnes.*

*Enter [Armado, the] Braggart, and [Moth,] his Boy.*    III, i

*Armado.* Warble, child; make passionate my sense of
    hearing.
*Moth. [sings]* Concolinel.
*Armado.* Sweet air! Go, tenderness of years, take this key,
    give enlargement to the swain, bring him festinately 5
    hither. I must employ him in a letter to my love.
*Moth.* Master, will you win your love with a French brawl?
*Armado.* How meanest thou? Brawling in French?
*Moth.* No, my complete master; but to jig off a tune at the
    tongue's end, canary to it with your feet, humor it with 10
    turning up your eyelids, sigh a note and sing a note, some-

---

III, i, 1 *make passionate* render responsive  3 *Concolinel* (unidentified;
possibly the name or refrain of a song)  5 *festinately* quickly  7 *brawl* (a
figure dance)  10 *canary* dance with improvisations

time through the throat as if you swallowed love by singing love, sometime through the nose as if you snuffed up
love by smelling love; with your hat penthouse-like o'er
15 the shop of your eyes; with your arms crossed on your
thin-belly doublet like a rabbit on a spit; or your hands in
your pocket like a man after the old painting; and keep
not too long in one tune, but a snip and away. These are
complements, these are humors, these betray nice wenches
20 (that would be betrayed without these), and make them
men of note—do you note—men that most are affected
to these.
*Armado.* How hast thou purchased this experience?
*Moth.* By my penny of observation.
25 *Armado.* But O — but O —
*Moth.* The hobby-horse is forgot.
*Armado.* Call'st thou my love 'hobby-horse'?
*Moth.* No, master; the hobby-horse is but a colt, and your
love perhaps a hackney. But have you forgot your love?
30 *Armado.* Almost I had.
*Moth.* Negligent student! learn her by heart.
*Armado.* By heart, and in heart, boy.
*Moth.* And out of heart, master. All those three I will prove.
*Armado.* What wilt thou prove?
35 *Moth.* A man, if I live; and this, by, in, and without, upon
the instant. By heart you love her, because your heart
cannot come by her; in heart you love her, because your
heart is in love with her; and out of heart you love her,
being out of heart that you cannot enjoy her.

14 *penthouse* (an overhang, such as often sheltered shops)  15–16 *on . . .
doublet* i.e. on the doublet covering your thin belly  17 *old painting* (unidentified)  18 *snip* snippet, scrap  19 *complements* accomplishments *humors* mannerisms  *nice* coy  21 *affected* drawn, given  25–26 *But O . . .
forgot* (refrain of a popular song)  27–29 *hobby-horse, colt, hackney* (cant
terms for prostitutes)

*Armado.* I am all these three. 40

*Moth. [aside]* And three times as much more, and yet
nothing at all.

*Armado.* Fetch hither the swain. He must carry me a letter.

*Moth. [aside]* A message well sympathized — a horse to be
ambassador for an ass. 45

*Armado.* Ha, ha? what sayest thou?

*Moth.* Marry, sir, you must send the ass upon the horse, for
he is very slow-gaited. But I go.

*Armado.* The way is but short. Away!

*Moth.* As swift as lead, sir. 50

*Armado.* The meaning, pretty ingenious?
Is not lead a metal heavy, dull, and slow?

*Moth.* Minime, honest master; or rather, master, no.

*Armado.* I say, lead is slow.

*Moth.* You are too swift, sir, to say so.
Is that lead slow which is fired from a gun? 55

*Armado.* Sweet smoke of rhetoric!
He reputes me a cannon; and the bullet, that's he:
I shoot thee at the swain.

*Moth.* Thump, then, and I flee. *[Exit.]*

*Armado.* A most acute juvenal; voluble and free of grace!
By thy favor, sweet welkin, I must sigh in thy face: 60
Most rude melancholy, valor gives thee place.
My herald is returned.

*Enter [Moth, the] Page, and [Costard, the] Clown.*

*Moth.* A wonder, master! Here's a costard broken in a shin.

---

43 *me* for me    44 *sympathized* harmonized    53 *Minime* by no means
(Latin)    56 *smoke* product, essence    58 *Thump* (equivalent to 'bang')    59
*juvenal* youth    60 *By thy favor* with your permission    *welkin* sky    61 *gives
thee place* gives place to you, i.e. to melancholy    63 *costard* apple or head
(and hence having no shin)

*Armado.* Some enigma, some riddle. Come, thy l'envoy —
    begin.

65 *Costard.* No egma, no riddle, no l'envoy; no salve in the
    mail, sir. O, sir, plantain, a plain plantain. No l'envoy, no
    l'envoy, no salve, sir, but a plantain.

*Armado.* By virtue, thou enforcest laughter; thy silly
    thought, my spleen; the heaving of my lungs provokes
70     me to ridiculous smiling. O, pardon me, my stars! Doth
    the inconsiderate take salve for l'envoy, and the word
    l'envoy for a salve?

*Moth.* Do the wise think them other? Is not l'envoy a salve?

*Armado.* No, page; it is an epilogue, or discourse to make
    plain
75 Some obscure precedence that hath tofore been sain.
    I will example it:
        The fox, the ape, and the humble-bee
        Were still at odds, being but three.
    There's the moral. Now the l'envoy.

80 *Moth.* I will add the l'envoy. Say the moral again.

*Armado.* The fox, the ape, and the humble-bee
        Were still at odds, being but three.

*Moth.*     Until the goose came out of door,
        And stayed the odds by adding four.

85 Now will I begin your moral, and do you follow with
    my l'envoy.
        The fox, the ape, and the humble-bee
        Were still at odds, being but three.

---

64 *l'envoy* (a commentary or injunction concluding a literary composition)
65 *salve* (the play seems to be on 'salve'—salute—suggested by 'l'envoy')
66 *mail* pouch (such as might be carried by a salve-vendor or quacksalver
*plantain* (a homely herbal remedy for broken shins) 69 *spleen* risibility
(laughter supposedly originated in the spleen) 71 *inconsiderate* i.e. un-
thinking one 75 *precedence* preceding discourse  *sain* said  84 *stayed*
wiped out  *four* a fourth

*Armado.*Until the goose came out of door,
     Staying the odds by adding four.       90

*Moth.* A good l'envoy, ending in the goose. Would you
  desire more?

*Costard.* The boy hath sold him a bargain, a goose — that's
  flat.

  Sir, your pennyworth is good, an your goose be fat.

  To sell a bargain well is as cunning as fast and loose.   95

  Let me see — a fat l'envoy — ay, that's a fat goose.

*Armado.* Come hither, come hither. How did this argument
  begin?

*Moth.* By saying that a costard was broken in a shin.
  Then called you for the l'envoy.

*Costard.* True, and I for a plantain; thus came your argument in;          100

  Then the boy's fat l'envoy, the goose that you bought;

  And he ended the market.

*Armado.* But tell me, how was there a costard broken in a
  shin?

*Moth.* I will tell you sensibly.         105

*Costard.* Thou hast no feeling of it, Moth. I will speak that
  l'envoy:

  I, Costard, running out, that was safely within,

  Fell over the threshold and broke my shin.

*Armado.* We will talk no more of this matter.     110

*Costard.* Till there be more matter in the shin.

*Armado.* Sirrah Costard, I will enfranchise thee.

*Costard.* O, marry me to one Frances! I smell some l'envoy,
  some goose, in this.

89 *goose* i.e. Armado (who has been tricked into the rôle)  93 *sold . . .
bargain* i.e. outwitted him  94 *your . . . good* i.e. you got your money's
worth  *an* if  95 *fast and loose* (cf. I, ii, 146)  97 *argument* topic, theme
105 *sensibly* feelingly  111 *matter* pus  112 *enfranchise* free

115 *Armado.* By my sweet soul, I mean setting thee at liberty,
enfreedoming thy person. Thou wert immured, re-
strained, captivated, bound.

*Costard.* True, true, and now you will be my purgation and
let me loose.

120 *Armado.* I give thee thy liberty, set thee from durance; and
in lieu thereof, impose on thee nothing but this. *[Gives a
letter.]* Bear this significant to the country maid — Jaquenetta. *[Gives money.]* There is remuneration; for the best
ward of mine honor is rewarding my dependents. Moth,

125 follow.                                                    *[Exit.]*

*Moth.* Like the sequel, I. Signior Costard, adieu.       *Exit.*

*Costard.* My sweet ounce of man's flesh, my incony Jew!
Now will I look to his remuneration. Remuneration?
O that's the Latin word for three farthings. Three far-

130 things — remuneration. 'What's the price of this inkle?'
'One penny.' 'No, I'll give you a remuneration.' Why, it
carries it! Remuneration! Why, it is a fairer name than
French crown. I will never buy and sell out of this word.

*Enter Berowne.*

*Berowne.* O my good knave Costard, exceedingly well met.

135 *Costard.* Pray you, sir, how much carnation ribbon may a
man buy for a remuneration?

*Berowne.* O, what is a remuneration?

*Costard.* Marry, sir, halfpenny farthing.

*Berowne.* O, why then, three-farthing-worth of silk.

140 *Costard.* I thank your worship. God be wi' you.

*Berowne.* O stay, slave; I must employ thee.

122 *significant* communication   124 *ward* defense   127 *incony* darling
*Jew* (a term of playful abuse, perhaps suggested by 'juvenile')   130 *inkle*
tape   132 *carries it* takes the prize   133 *French crown* (a coin, frequently
associated with jests about venereal disease)   *out of* i.e. without using   135
*carnation* flesh-colored

As thou wilt win my favor, good my knave,
Do one thing for me that I shall entreat.
*Costard.* When would you have it done, sir?
*Berowne.* O, this afternoon. 145
*Costard.* Well, I will do it, sir. Fare you well.
*Berowne.* O, thou knowest not what it is.
*Costard.* I shall know, sir, when I have done it.
*Berowne.* Why, villain, thou must know first.
*Costard.* I will come to your worship to-morrow morning. 150
*Berowne.* It must be done this afternoon. Hark, slave, it is
but this:
The princess comes to hunt here in the park,
And in her train there is a gentle lady —
When tongues speak sweetly, then they name her name, 155
And Rosaline they call her. Ask for her,
And to her white hand see thou do commend
This sealed-up counsel. *[Gives letter and a shilling.]* There's
thy guerdon: go.
*Costard.* Gardon, O sweet gardon! Better than remunera-
tion — a 'leven-pence farthing better. Most sweet gardon! 160
I will do it, sir, in print. Gardon — remuneration. *Exit.*
*Berowne.* O, and I, forsooth, in love!
I, that have been love's whip,
A very beadle to a humorous sigh,
A critic, nay, a night-watch constable, 165
A domineering pedant o'er the boy,
Than whom no mortal so magnificent.
This wimpled, whining, purblind, wayward boy,
This senior-junior, giant-dwarf, Dan Cupid,

---

158 *counsel* private message *guerdon* reward   161 *in print* i.e. to the letter
164 *beadle . . . sigh* i.e. an officer of correction to symptoms of love   166
*pedant* schoolmaster   168 *wimpled* veiled   *purblind* wholly blind   169 *Dan*
don, sir (from 'dominus')

170    Regent of love-rimes, lord of folded arms,
       The anointed sovereign of sighs and groans,
       Liege of all loiterers and malcontents,
       Dread prince of plackets, king of codpieces,
       Sole imperator and great general
175    Of trotting paritors — O my little heart!
       And I to be a corporal of his field,
       And wear his colors like a tumbler's hoop!
       What? I love, I sue, I seek a wife!
       A woman that is like a German clock,
180    Still a-repairing, ever out of frame,
       And never going aright, being a watch,
       But being watched that it may still go right!
       Nay, to be perjured, which is worst of all;
       And, among three, to love the worst of all;
185    A whitely wanton with a velvet brow,
       With two pitch balls stuck in her face for eyes.
       Ay, and, by heaven, one that will do the deed,
       Though Argus were her eunuch and her guard.
       And I to sigh for her, to watch for her,
190    To pray for her! Go to, it is a plague
       That Cupid will impose for my neglect
       Of his almighty dreadful little might.
       Well, I will love, write, sigh, pray, sue, groan:
       Some men must love my lady, and some Joan.    *[Exit.]*

❈

170 *folded arms* (traditional posture of the melancholy lover)   172 *Liege*
lord   173 *plackets* slits in petticoats   *codpieces* padded gussets at the crotch
of breeches (like 'placket,' often used in ribald allusion)   175 *paritors*
minor officers of ecclesiastical courts who profited by spying out sexual
offenses   177 *tumbler's hoop* (an object conspicuously beribboned)   180
*frame* order   185 *whitely* pale-skinned   188 *Argus* (in mythology a monster with a thousand eyes)   *eunuch* (guard in a seraglio)   189 *watch* stay
awake   194 *Joan* (proverbial name for an ordinary woman)

*Enter the Princess, a Forester, her Ladies [Maria,*
*Katharine, Rosaline], and her Lords [Boyet and others].*

*Princess.* Was that the king, that spurred his horse so hard
    Against the steep uprising of the hill?
*Boyet.* I know not, but I think it was not he.
*Princess.* Whoe'er 'a was, 'a showed a mounting mind.
    Well, lords, to-day we shall have our dispatch;       5
    On Saturday we will return to France.
    Then, forester, my friend, where is the bush
    That we must stand and play the murderer in?
*Forester.* Hereby, upon the edge of yonder coppice,
    A stand where you may make the fairest shoot.      10
*Princess.* I thank my beauty, I am fair that shoot,
    And thereupon thou speak'st the fairest shoot.
*Forester.* Pardon me, madam, for I meant not so.
*Princess.* What, what? First praise me, and again say no?
    O short-lived pride! Not fair? Alack for woe!      15
*Forester.* Yes, madam, fair.
*Princess.*                  Nay, never paint me now:
    Where fair is not, praise cannot mend the brow.
    Here, good my glass, take this for telling true –
                        *[Gives money.]*
    Fair payment for foul words is more than due.
*Forester.* Nothing but fair is that which you inherit.      20
*Princess.* See, see – my beauty will be saved by merit.
    O heresy in fair, fit for these days,
    A giving hand, though foul, shall have fair praise.

IV, i, 10 *stand* (concealed position toward which the game was driven)
16 *paint* flatter  17 *brow* i.e. face  18 *good my glass* my good mirror  20
*inherit* possess  21 *merit* i.e. good works, the 'alms' she has given the
forester  22 *heresy* (in orthodox Anglican doctrine salvation came by faith
rather than by good works)

But come, the bow. Now mercy goes to kill,
25 And shooting well is then accounted ill.
Thus will I save my credit in the shoot:
Not wounding, pity would not let me do 't;
If wounding, then it was to show my skill,
That more for praise than purpose meant to kill.
30 And out of question so it is sometimes,
Glory grows guilty of detested crimes,
When, for fame's sake, for praise, an outward part,
We bend to that the working of the heart;
As I for praise alone now seek to spill
35 The poor deer's blood, that my heart means no ill.
*Boyet.* Do not curst wives hold that self-sovereignty
Only for praise' sake, when they strive to be
Lords o'er their lords?
*Princess.* Only for praise; and praise we may afford
40 To any lady that subdues a lord.

### Enter [Costard, the] Clown.

*Boyet.* Here comes a member of the commonwealth.
*Costard.* God dig-you-den all. Pray you, which is the head
    lady?
*Princess.* Thou shalt know her, fellow, by the rest that have
45 no heads.
*Costard.* Which is the greatest lady, the highest?
*Princess.* The thickest and the tallest.
*Costard.* The thickest and the tallest — it is so. Truth is truth.

---

24 *mercy . . . kill* i.e. to the merciful huntsman good shooting (which only
wounded so that the kill might be left to the dogs) is ill doing  29 *That
. . . kill* i.e. who shot well to win praise rather than from any desire to strike
the deer  31 *Glory . . . of* i.e. desire for glory is responsible for  32 *an
outward part* a superficial thing  33 *bend* adapt  36 *curst* shrewish  *self-
sovereignty* self-rule (instead of rule by their husbands)  41 *commonwealth*
citizenry  42 *dig-you-den* give you good evening

An your waist, mistress, were as slender as my wit,
One o' these maids' girdles for your waist should be fit.   50
Are not you the chief woman? You are the thickest here.

*Princess.* What's your will, sir? What's your will?

*Costard.* I have a letter from Monsieur Berowne to one
Lady Rosaline.

*Princess.* O thy letter, thy letter! He's a good friend of mine.   55
Stand aside, good bearer. Boyet, you can carve;
Break up this capon.

*Boyet.*                    I am bound to serve.
This letter is mistook; it importeth none here.
It is writ to Jaquenetta.

*Princess.*                    We will read it, I swear.
Break the neck of the wax, and every one give ear.   60

*Boyet.* (*reads*) 'By heaven, that thou art fair is most infallible;
true that thou art beauteous; truth itself that thou art
lovely. More fairer than fair, beautiful than beauteous,
truer than truth itself, have commiseration on thy heroical
vassal. The magnanimous and most illustrate king Co-   65
phetua set eye upon the pernicious and indubitate beggar
Zenelophon, and he it was that might rightly say veni,
vidi, vici; which to anathomize in the vulgar (O base and
obscure vulgar!) videlicet, he came, saw, and overcame.
He came, one; saw, two; overcame, three. Who came?   70
The king. Why did he come? To see. Why did he see?
To overcome. To whom came he? To the beggar. What
saw he? The beggar. Who overcame he? The beggar.
The conclusion is victory. On whose side? The king's.
The captive is enriched. On whose side? The beggar's.   75

---

57 *capon* love-letter (from French slang—'poulet')   58 *importeth* concerns
60 *wax* seal   65 *illustrate* illustrious   66 *indubitate* indubitable   67 *Zenelophon* (Penelophon, in the old ballad of 'King Cophetua and the Beggar-
maid')   68 *anathomize* anatomize, parse

The catastrophe is a nuptial. On whose side? The king's?
No — on both in one, or one in both. I am the king (for
so stands the comparison), thou the beggar (for so wit-
nesseth thy lowliness). Shall I command thy love? I may.
80 Shall I enforce thy love? I could. Shall I entreat thy love?
I will. What shalt thou exchange for rags? Robes. For
tittles? Titles. For thyself? Me. Thus, expecting thy
reply, I profane my lips on thy foot, my eyes on thy picture, and my heart on thy every part.
85      Thine in the dearest design of industry,
                         Don Adriano de Armado.
Thus dost thou hear the Nemean lion roar
     'Gainst thee, thou lamb, that standest as his prey.
Submissive fall his princely feet before,
90      And he from forage will incline to play.
But if thou strive, poor soul, what art thou then?
Food for his rage, repasture for his den.'
*Princess.* What plume of feathers is he that indited this
     letter?
     What vane? What weathercock? Did you ever hear
     better?
95 *Boyet.* I am much deceived but I remember the style.
*Princess.* Else your memory is bad, going o'er it erewhile.
*Boyet.* This Armado is a Spaniard that keeps here in court;
     A phantasime, a Monarcho, and one that makes sport
     To the prince and his book-mates.

76 *catastrophe* denouement   82 *tittles* jots, particles   85 *dearest ... industry*
i.e. best pattern of assiduous courtship   87 *Nemean lion* (slain by Hercules
as the first of his labors)   90 *forage* foraging, ravaging   92 *repasture* repast
93 *plume of feathers* i.e. dandy, coxcomb   94 *vane* weather-vane (with play
on 'vain')   96 *erewhile* just now   97 *keeps* dwells   98 *phantasime* one who
indulges in fantasies   *Monarcho* (the nickname of an Italian eccentric whose
delusions of grandeur entertained the English court for some years prior to
1580)

*Princess.*                                    Thou fellow, a word.
  Who gave thee this letter?
*Costard.*                          I told you — my lord.              100
*Princess.* To whom shouldst thou give it?
*Costard.*                          From my lord to my lady.
*Princess.* From which lord, to which lady?
*Costard.* From my lord Berowne, a good master of mine,
  To a lady of France, that he called Rosaline.
*Princess.* Thou hast mistaken his letter. Come, lords,
    away.                                                             105
  Here, sweet, put up this; 'twill be thine another day.
                    *Exeunt [Princess, Forester, and Attendants].*
*Boyet.* Who is the suitor? Who is the suitor?
*Rosaline.*                          Shall I teach you to know?
*Boyet.* Ay, my continent of beauty.
*Rosaline.*                          Why, she that bears the bow.
  Finely put off!
*Boyet.* My lady goes to kill horns, but, if thou marry,             110
  Hang me by the neck if horns that year miscarry.
  Finely put on!
*Rosaline.* Well then, I am the shooter.
*Boyet.*                          And who is your deer?
*Rosaline.* If we choose by the horns, yourself. Come not
    near.
  Finely put on, indeed!                                             115
*Maria.* You still wrangle with her, Boyet, and she strikes
  at the brow.
*Boyet.* But she herself is hit lower. Have I hit her now?
*Rosaline.* Shall I come upon thee with an old saying that

---

105 *mistaken* wrongly delivered  106 *'twill be thine* i.e. you will send one
like it  107 *suitor* (pronounced 'shooter')  108 *continent of* container of all
109 *put off* turned aside  110 *horns* i.e. a deer (followed by an allusion to the
horns of cuckoldry)  118 *come upon thee* confront you

was a man when King Pepin of France was a little boy, as
120    touching the hit it?

*Boyet.* So I may answer thee with one as old — that was a
woman when Queen Guinever of Britain was a little
wench, as touching the hit it.

*Rosaline.* 'Thou canst not hit it, hit it, hit it,
125              Thou canst not hit it, my good man.

*Boyet.*       'An I cannot, cannot, cannot,
               An I cannot, another can.'        *Exit [Rosaline].*

*Costard.* By my troth, most pleasant, how both did fit it!

*Maria.* A mark marvellous well shot, for they both did
hit it.

*Boyet.* A mark! (O mark but that mark!) A mark, says my
130    lady!
Let the mark have a prick in 't, to mete at if it may be.

*Maria.* Wide o' the bow hand! I' faith your hand is out.

*Costard.* Indeed 'a must shoot nearer, or he'll ne'er hit the
clout.

*Boyet.* An if my hand be out, then belike your hand is in.

135 *Costard.* Then will she get the upshoot by cleaving the pin.

*Maria.* Come, come, you talk greasily; your lips grow foul.

*Costard.* She's too hard for you at pricks. Sir, challenge her
to bowl.

*Boyet.* I fear too much rubbing. Good night, my good owl.
               *[Exeunt Boyet and Maria.]*

*Costard.* By my soul, a swain, a most simple clown!
140    Lord, lord, how the ladies and I have put him down!

119 *was a man* i.e. was old   *King Pepin* (Carlovingian king who died in 768)
124–27 *Thou . . . can* (adapted from a ribald song and dance of the period)
129 *mark* target   131 *prick* (center point or strip in the target)   *mete at*
measure by   132 *Wide . . . hand* too far left   133 *clout* white-headed pin in
center of target   135 *upshoot* leading shot in a contest   136 *greasily*
grossly (referring to double-entendres preceding)   137 *pricks* informal or
illegal archery   138 *rubbing* grazing (a bowling term)

O' my troth, most sweet jests, most incony vulgar wit!
When it comes so smoothly off, so obscenely as it were,
    so fit.
Armado o' th' t'one side – O, a most dainty man!
To see him walk before a lady, and to bear her fan,
To see him kiss his hand, and how most sweetly 'a will
    swear;                                                        145
And his page o' t'other side, that handful of wit,
Ah, heavens, it is a most pathetical nit!    *Shout within.*
Sola, sola!                                        *[Exit.]*

*Enter Dull, Holofernes the Pedant, and Nathaniel.*    IV, ii

*Nathaniel.* Very reverend sport, truly, and done in the testi-
    mony of a good conscience.
*Holofernes.* The deer was, as you know, sanguis, in blood;
    ripe as the pomewater, who now hangeth like a jewel in
    the ear of coelo, the sky, the welkin, the heaven; and anon  5
    falleth like a crab on the face of terra, the soil, the land,
    the earth.
*Nathaniel.* Truly, Master Holofernes, the epithets are
    sweetly varied, like a scholar at the least; but, sir, I assure
    ye it was a buck of the first head.                          10

141 *incony* darling  *vulgar* popular (?)  142 *obscenely* (unconsciously apt
malapropism—for 'seemly'?)  143–147 *Armado . . . nit* (unless Costard is
simply recalling something he has previously observed offstage, this un-
expected reference to Armado and Moth may indicate a gap in the present
version of the scene)  147 *pathetical nit* pleasing mite  148 *Sola, sola* (a
hunting cry)  IV, ii, 1 *reverend* revered  1–2 *in the testimony* with the warrant  3 *in blood* in prime condition  4 *pomewater* (a variety of apple)
6 *crab* crab-apple  9 *at the least* to say the least  10 *of . . . head* of the fifth
year (and therefore a 'buck'; Holofernes has called it a 'deer')

*Holofernes.* Sir Nathaniel, haud credo.

*Dull.* 'Twas not a haud credo; 'twas a pricket.

*Holofernes.* Most barbarous intimation! Yet a kind of insinuation, as it were, in via, in way, of explication; facere,
15 as it were, replication, or rather, ostentare, to show, as it were, his inclination — after his undressed, unpolished, uneducated, unpruned, untrained, or, rather, unlettered, or, ratherest, unconfirmed fashion — to insert again my haud credo for a deer.

20 *Dull.* I said the deer was not a haud credo — 'twas a pricket.

*Holofernes.* Twice sod simplicity, bis coctus!

O thou monster Ignorance, how deformèd dost thou look!

*Nathaniel.* Sir, he hath not fed of the dainties that are bred in a book.

He hath not eat paper, as it were; he hath not drunk ink.
25 His intellect is not replenished; he is only an animal, only sensible in the duller parts.

And such barren plants are set before us that we thankful should be,

Which we of taste and feeling are, for those parts that do fructify in us more than he;

For as it would ill become me to be vain, indiscreet, or a fool:

So were there a patch set on learning, to see him in a
30 school.

11 *Sir* dominus (term of address for a clergyman in minor orders) *haud credo* I do not think so  12 *not . . . credo* (Dull has mistaken the Latin 'credo' for a reference to some kind of 'doe')  *pricket* (male deer of the second year)  13 *intimation* intrusion  13–14 *insinuation* interpretation  14–15 *facere . . . replication* to give another explanation (Holofernes' words, exploiting presumed literal meanings, may be called 'pedanticisms')  18 *insert* put in, interpret  21 *sod* sodden  *bis coctus* twice-cooked, sodden  28 *Which we* we who  *fructify* grow fruitful  *he* in him  30 *patch . . . learning* (1) disfigurement of education (2) clown put to school

But, omne bene, say I, being of an old father's mind,
Many can brook the weather that love not the wind.

*Dull.* You two are book-men. Can you tell me by your wit,
What was a month old at Cain's birth that's not five
weeks old as yet?

*Holofernes.* Dictynna, goodman Dull. Dictynna, goodman
Dull.                                                          35

*Dull.* What is Dictynna?

*Nathaniel.* A title to Phoebe, to Luna, to the moon.

*Holofernes.* The moon was a month old when Adam was
no more,

And raught not to five weeks when he came to five-
score.

Th' allusion holds in the exchange.                            40

*Dull.* 'Tis true indeed; the collusion holds in the exchange.

*Holofernes.* God comfort thy capacity! I say th' allusion
holds in the exchange.

*Dull.* And I say the pollusion holds in the exchange, for the
moon is never but a month old; and I say beside that 'twas   45
a pricket that the princess killed.

*Holofernes.* Sir Nathaniel, will you hear an extemporal epi-
taph on the death of the deer? And, to humor the ignorant, call I the deer the princess killed, a pricket.

*Nathaniel.* Perge, good Master Holofernes, perge, so it shall  50
please you to abrogate scurrility.

*Holofernes.* I will something affect the letter, for it argues
facility.

The preyful princess pierced and pricked a pretty pleasing
pricket;

31 *omne bene* all's well *father's* sage's  32 *brook* put up with (i.e. what
can't be cured must be endured)  35 *Dictynna* Diana, the moon  39 *raught*
reached  40 *allusion* dark saying, riddle  *exchange* substitution (of Adam's
name for Cain's)  47 *extemporal* extemporary  50 *Perge* proceed  52
*affect the letter* i.e. lean to the use of alliteration

Some say a sore, but not a sore till now made sore with
55     shooting.
The dogs did yell. Put l to sore, then sorel jumps from
       thicket;
Or pricket, sore, or else sorel. The people fall a hooting.
If sore be sore, then l to sore makes fifty sores – O sore l!
Of one sore I an hundred make by adding but one
       more l.

60 *Nathaniel.* A rare talent!

*Dull.* If a talent be a claw, look how he claws him with a
talent.

*Holofernes.* This is a gift that I have, simple, simple; a foolish
extravagant spirit, full of forms, figures, shapes, objects,
65     ideas, apprehensions, motions, revolutions. These are
begot in the ventricle of memory, nourished in the womb
of pia mater, and delivered upon the mellowing of occasion. But the gift is good in those in whom it is acute,
and I am thankful for it.

70 *Nathaniel.* Sir, I praise the Lord for you, and so may my
parishioners; for their sons are well tutored by you, and
their daughters profit very greatly under you. You are a
good member of the commonwealth.

*Holofernes.* Mehercle, if their sons be ingenious, they shall
75     want no instruction; if their daughters be capable, I will
put it to them. But, *vir sapit qui pauca loquitur.* A soul
feminine saluteth us.

---

55 *sore* (deer of the fourth year)   56 *sorel* (deer of the third year)   57 *Or*
either   58 *l* (roman numeral fifty)   61 *talent* i.e. talon   *claws* scratches,
flatters   66 *ventricle* (of the three sections or 'ventricles' of the brain one
was believed to contain the memory)   66–67 *womb ... pia mater* center of
the enclosing membrane or purse   74 *Mehercle* by Hercules   75 *capable*
(1) able   (2) sexually mature (operating with other double-entendres of
the passage)   76 *vir ... loquitur* the man is wise who speaks little

*Enter Jaquenetta and [Costard,] the Clown.*

*Jaquenetta.* God give you good morrow, Master Parson.

*Holofernes.* Master Parson, *quasi* pers-one? And if one
    should be pierced, which is the one?          80

*Costard.* Marry, Master Schoolmaster, he that is likest to a
    hogshead.

*Holofernes.* Of piercing a hogshead! A good lustre of con-
    ceit in a turf of earth, fire enough for a flint, pearl enough
    for a swine — 'tis pretty, it is well.          85

*Jaquenetta.* Good Master Parson, be so good as read me this
    letter. It was given me by Costard, and sent me from Don
    Armado. I beseech you read it.

*Holofernes.* Facile precor gelida quando pecas omnia sub
    umbra ruminat, and so forth. Ah, good old Mantuan. I  90
    may speak of thee as the traveller doth of Venice:

             Venechia, Venechia,
          Que non te vede, que non te prechia.

    Old Mantuan, old Mantuan! Who understandeth thee
    not, loves thee not. Ut, re, sol, la, mi, fa. Under pardon,  95
    sir, what are the contents? or, rather, as Horace says in
    his — What my soul! Verses?

*Nathaniel.* Ay, sir, and very learned.

*Holofernes.* Let me hear a staff, a stanze, a verse. Lege,
    domine.          100

---

78 *Parson* (pronounced 'person') 79 *quasi* that is 80 *pierced* (pronounced
'persed') 83–84 *lustre of conceit* gleam of fancy 89–90 *Facile . . . ruminat*
(a misquotation of the opening of the first eclogue of Mantuanus—a common school tag: 'Fauste, precor gelida quando pecus omne sub umbra ruminat': Faustus, I beg, while all the cattle ruminate beneath the cool shade)
92–93 *Venechia . . . prechia* (rugged form of an Italian proverb appearing in
Florio's *First Fruits,* 1578: Venice, Venice, who loves you not sees you not)
95 *Ut* (since replaced by 'do'; Holofernes is incorrectly singing the scale)
99–100 *Lege, domine* read, master

*Nathaniel.* *[reads]* 'If love make me forsworn, how shall I
    swear to love?
    Ah, never faith could hold if not to beauty vowed!
Though to myself forsworn, to thee I'll faithful prove;
    Those thoughts to me were oaks, to thee like osiers
    bowed.

105 Study his bias leaves and makes his book thine eyes,
    Where all those pleasures live that art would compre-
    hend.
If knowledge be the mark, to know thee shall suffice:
    Well learnèd is that tongue that well can thee commend,
All ignorant that soul that sees thee without wonder;

110     Which is to me some praise, that I thy parts admire.
Thy eye Jove's lightning bears, thy voice his dreadful
    thunder,
    Which, not to anger bent, is music and sweet fire.
Celestial as thou art, O pardon love this wrong,
    That sings heaven's praise with such an earthly tongue!'

115 *Holofernes.* You find not the apostrophus, and so miss the
accent. Let me supervise the canzonet. Here are only numbers ratified; but, for the elegancy, facility, and golden ca-
dence of poesy, caret. Ovidius Naso was the man; and
why indeed 'Naso' but for smelling out the odoriferous
120 flowers of fancy, the jerks of invention? Imitari is nothing. So doth the hound his master, the ape his keeper, the

---

104 *thoughts ... were* resolutions which seemed to me   105 *his bias leaves*
i.e. abandons its previous inclinations   110 *praise* credit, honor   115 *find*
regard   *apostrophus* apostrophe (disregarding contractions indicated by
apostrophes can spoil the meter, but perhaps Holofernes is using learned
terms at random)   116 *supervise* look over   *canzonet* ditty   116-17 *numbers ratified* i.e. mechanical versification   118 *caret* it is lacking   *Naso*
(from 'nasus,' nose)   120 *jerks of invention* strokes of wit   *Imitari* to imitate

tired horse his rider. But, damosella virgin, was this directed to you?

*Jaquenetta.* Ay, sir, from one Monsieur Berowne, one of the strange queen's lords. 125

*Holofernes.* I will overglance the superscript. 'To the snow-white hand of the most beauteous Lady Rosaline.' I will look again on the intellect of the letter, for the nomination of the party writing to the person written unto. 'Your ladyship's, in all desired employment, Berowne.' 130 Sir Nathaniel, this Berowne is one of the votaries with the king; and here he hath framed a letter to a sequent of the stranger queen's, which accidentally, or by the way of progression, hath miscarried. Trip and go, my sweet; deliver this paper into the royal hand of the king; it may 135 concern much. Stay not thy compliment; I forgive thy duty. Adieu.

*Jaquenetta.* Good Costard, go with me. Sir, God save your life.

*Costard.* Have with thee, my girl. *Exit [with Jaquenetta].* 140

*Nathaniel.* Sir, you have done this in the fear of God very religiously; and, as a certain father saith —

*Holofernes.* Sir, tell not me of the father; I do fear colorable colors. But to return to the verses — did they please you, Sir Nathaniel? 145

*Nathaniel.* Marvellous well for the pen.

*Holofernes.* I do dine to-day at the father's of a certain pupil of mine, where, if before repast it shall please you to grat-

---

122 *tired* spiritless (Holofernes seems to be linking imitativeness and docility) 125 *strange* foreign (but Berowne, contrary to Jaquenetta's remark, is native) 126 *superscript* address 128 *intellect* final rhetorical flourish (?) 132 *sequent* follower 133–34 *by . . . progression* i.e. en route 136 *Stay . . . compliment* i.e. do not stand on ceremony 143–44 *colorable colors* plausible pretexts 146 *pen* style (as contrasted with content)

ify the table with a grace, I will, on my privilege I have
150   with the parents of the foresaid child or pupil, undertake
your ben venuto; where I will prove those verses to be
very unlearned, neither savoring of poetry, wit, nor invention. I beseech your society.

*Nathaniel.* And thank you too, for society (saith the text) is
155   the happiness of life.

*Holofernes.* And, certes, the text most infallibly concludes
it. *[to Dull]* Sir, I do invite you too; you shall not say me
nay. Pauca verba. Away! The gentles are at their game,
and we will to our recreation.                    *Exeunt.*

IV, iii          *Enter Berowne with a paper in his hand, alone.*

*Berowne.* The king he is hunting the deer; I am coursing
myself. They have pitched a toil; I am toiling in a pitch
— pitch that defiles. Defile — a foul word! Well, set thee
down, sorrow, for so they say the fool said, and so say I,
5     and I the fool. Well proved, wit! By the Lord, this love is
as mad as Ajax: it kills sheep; it kills me — I a sheep. Well
proved again o' my side! I will not love; if I do, hang me.
I' faith, I will not. O but her eye! By this light, but for her
eye, I would not love her — yes, for her two eyes. Well, I
10    do nothing in the world but lie, and lie in my throat. By
heaven, I do love, and it hath taught me to rime, and to be
mallicholy; and here is part of my rime, and here my mel-

---

151 *ben venuto* welcome   154 *text* (unidentified)   158 *Pauca verba* few
words   IV, iii, 2 *pitched a toil* set a snare   3–4 *set . . . sorrow* (cf. I, i, 297)   6
*Ajax* (legendary Greek warrior who ran mad and mistook sheep for an
army after he failed to be awarded the armor of Achilles)   12 *mallicholy*
melancholy

ancholy. Well, she hath one o' my sonnets already. The
clown bore it, the fool sent it, and the lady hath it — sweet
clown, sweeter fool, sweetest lady! By the world, I would 15
not care a pin if the other three were in. Here comes one
with a paper: God give him grace to groan!

*He stands aside.*

*The King ent'reth [with a paper].*

*King.* Ay me!
*Berowne. [aside]* Shot, by heaven! Proceed, sweet Cupid;
thou hast thumped him with thy bird-bolt under the left 20
pap. In faith, secrets!
*King. [reads]* 'So sweet a kiss the golden sun gives not
　　To those fresh morning drops upon the rose,
As thy eye-beams when their fresh rays have smote
　　The night of dew that on my cheeks down flows. 25
Nor shines the silver moon one half so bright
　　Through the transparent bosom of the deep
As doth thy face, through tears of mine, give light.
　　Thou shin'st in every tear that I do weep;
No drop but as a coach doth carry thee; 30
　　So ridest thou triumphing in my woe.
Do but behold the tears that swell in me,
　　And they thy glory through my grief will show;
But do not love thyself — then thou will keep
My tears for glasses and still make me weep. 35
O queen of queens, how far dost thou excel
No thought can think, nor tongue of mortal tell!'
How shall she know my griefs? I'll drop the paper.
Sweet leaves, shade folly. Who is he comes here?

16 *in* involved   19 *Proceed* i.e. rise in status   20 *bird-bolt* blunt arrow
20-21 *left pap* left breast (heart)   35 *glasses* mirrors   39 *shade* conceal

*Enter Longaville [with a paper]. The King steps aside.*

40      What, Longaville? and reading? Listen, ear.
     *Berowne.* Now, in thy likeness, one more fool appear!
     *Longaville.* Ay me, I am forsworn.
     *Berowne.* Why, he comes in like a perjure, wearing papers.
     *King.* In love, I hope — sweet fellowship in shame!
45      *Berowne.* One drunkard loves another of the name.
     *Longaville.* Am I the first that have been perjured so?
     *Berowne.* I could put thee in comfort — not by two that I
        know.
     Thou mak'st the triumviry, the corner-cap of society,
     The shape of love's Tyburn, that hangs up simplicity.
50      *Longaville.* I fear these stubborn lines lack power to move.
     O sweet Maria, empress of my love!
     These numbers will I tear, and write in prose.
     *Berowne.* O, rimes are guards on wanton Cupid's hose;
     Disfigure not his shop.
     *Longaville.*         This same shall go. *He reads the sonnet.*
55      'Did not the heavenly rhetoric of thine eye,
        'Gainst whom the world cannot hold argument,
     Persuade my heart to this false perjury?
     Vows for thee broke deserve not punishment.
     A woman I forswore, but I will prove,
60         Thou being a goddess, I forswore not thee.
     My vow was earthly, thou a heavenly love;
        Thy grace, being gained, cures all disgrace in me.

---

41 *in thy likeness* i.e. in the flesh   43 *perjure* perjurer   *wearing papers* i.e. exposed in the stocks and wearing the papers involved in his offense   48 *triumviry* triumvirate   48–49 *corner-cap . . . Tyburn* (an allusion to the three-cornered cap worn by Roman Catholic priests, such as Dr. Story, who was hanged at Tyburn in 1571 on gallows shaped as a triangle, and thereafter called 'Dr. Story's cap')   50 *stubborn* i.e. composed with difficulty   53 *guards* trimmings   54 *shop* (slang for 'codpiece')   62 *grace* favor

Vows are but breath, and breath a vapor is:
  Then thou, fair sun, which on my earth dost shine,
Exhal'st this vapor-vow; in thee it is.          65
  If broken then, it is no fault of mine;
If by me broke, what fool is not so wise
To lose an oath to win a paradise?'

*Berowne.* This is the liver-vein, which makes flesh a deity,
A green goose a goddess. Pure, pure idolatry.     70
God amend us, God amend! We are much out o' the
  way.

        *Enter Dumaine [with a paper].*

*Longaville.* By whom shall I send this? — Company? Stay.
                              *[Steps aside.]*
*Berowne.* All hid, all hid — an old infant play.
Like a demi-god here sit I in the sky,
And wretched fools' secrets heedfully o'er-eye.     75
More sacks to the mill — O heavens, I have my wish!
Dumaine transformed — four woodcocks in a dish!
*Dumaine.* O most divine Kate!
*Berowne.* O most profane coxcomb!
*Dumaine.* By heaven, the wonder in a mortal eye!     80
*Berowne.* By earth, she is not, corporal; there you lie.
*Dumaine.* Her amber hairs for foul have amber quoted.
*Berowne.* An amber-colored raven was well noted.
*Dumaine.* As upright as the cedar.

---

65 *Exhal'st* draws up, absorbs  69 *liver-vein* i.e. sentiment of the liver
(organ of passion)  70 *green goose* i.e. gosling, young girl  73 *infant play*
child's game  74 *in the sky* (Berowne is in an elevated position, perhaps in
the rear stage gallery)  76 *More ... mill* i.e. more work, more grain to be
ground  77 *woodcocks* (birds notable for stupidity)  81 *corporal* (cf.
III, i, 176)  82 *quoted* designated (i.e. her amber hair has made real amber
appear foul in comparison)  83 *well noted* accurately observed (sar-
casm)

*Berowne.*               Stoop, I say —
    Her shoulder is with child.
85 *Dumaine.*             As fair as day.
    *Berowne.* Ay, as some days, but then no sun must shine.
    *Dumaine.* O that I had my wish!
    *Longaville.*            And I had mine!
    *King.* And I mine too, good Lord!
    *Berowne.* Amen, so I had mine. Is not that a good word?
90 *Dumaine.* I would forget her, but a fever she
    Reigns in my blood, and will rememb'red be.
    *Berowne.* A fever in your blood? Why, then incision
    Would let her out in saucers. Sweet misprision!
    *Dumaine.* Once more I'll read the ode that I have writ.
95 *Berowne.* Once more I'll mark how love can vary wit.
                              *Dumaine reads his sonnet.*

    *Dumaine.* 'On a day (alack the day!)
              Love, whose month is ever May,
              Spied a blossom passing fair
              Playing in the wanton air.
100             Through the velvet leaves the wind,
              All unseen, can passage find;
              That the lover, sick to death,
              Wished himself the heaven's breath.
              Air, quoth he, thy cheeks may blow;
105             Air, would I might triumph so,
              But, alack, my hand is sworn
              Ne'er to pluck thee from thy thorn.
              Vow, alack, for youth unmeet,
              Youth so apt to pluck a sweet!
110            Do not call it sin in me,
              That I am forsworn for thee;

---

84 *Stoop* stooped, misshapen   85 *is with child* i.e. has a hump   92 *incision* (for bleeding)   93 *misprision* error   95 *vary* variegate   102 *That* so that

> Thou for whom Jove would swear
> Juno but an Ethiop were;
> And deny himself for Jove,
> Turning mortal for thy love.'                          115

This will I send, and something else more plain,
That shall express my true love's fasting pain.
O would the King, Berowne, and Longaville
Were lovers too! Ill, to example ill,
Would from my forehead wipe a perjured note,          120
For none offend where all alike do dote.

*Longaville.* [*advancing*] Dumaine, thy love is far from charity,
That in love's grief desir'st society.
You may look pale, but I should blush, I know,
To be o'erheard and taken napping so.                 125

*King.* [*advancing*] Come, sir, you blush! As his your case is such;
You chide at him, offending twice as much.
You do not love Maria! Longaville
Did never sonnet for her sake compile,
Nor never lay his wreathèd arms athwart               130
His loving bosom to keep down his heart.
I have been closely shrouded in this bush,
And marked you both, and for you both did blush.
I heard your guilty rimes, observed your fashion,
Saw sighs reek from you, noted well your passion.     135
Ay me! says one; O Jove! the other cries;
One, her hairs were gold; crystal, the other's eyes.
[*To Longaville*] You would for paradise break faith and troth;

---

113 *Ethiop* blackamoor (proverbially ugly)  114 *for* i.e. to be  117 *fasting*
hungering  119 *example* serve as example for  120 *note* mark  135 *reek*
breathe

    *[To Dumaine]* And Jove, for your love, would infringe an
       oath.
140  What will Berowne say when that he shall hear
    Faith infringèd, which such zeal did swear?
    How will he scorn! How will he spend his wit!
    How will he triumph, leap and laugh at it!
    For all the wealth that ever I did see,
145  I would not have him know so much by me.
  Berowne. *[advancing]* Now step I forth to whip hypocrisy.
    Ah, good my liege, I pray thee pardon me.
    Good heart, what grace hast thou, thus to reprove
    These worms for loving, that art most in love?
150  Your eyes do make no coaches; in your tears
    There is no certain princess that appears;
    You'll not be perjured, 'tis a hateful thing –
    Tush, none but minstrels like of sonneting!
    But are you not ashamed? Nay, are you not,
155  All three of you, to be thus much o'ershot?
    You found his mote; the king your mote did see;
    But I a beam do find in each of three.
    O what a scene of fool'ry have I seen,
    Of sighs, of groans, of sorrow, and of teen!
160  O me, with what strict patience have I sat,
    To see a king transformèd to a gnat;
    To see great Hercules whipping a gig,
    And profound Solomon to tune a jig,
    And Nestor play at push-pin with the boys,
165  And critic Timon laugh at idle toys!

145 *by* about   155 *o'ershot* worsted   156, 157 *mote, beam* i.e. small defect,
large defect (cf. Matthew 7:3–5; Luke 6:41–42)   159 *teen* grief   161 *gnat*
i.e. a small buzzing creature   162 *gig* top   163 *tune a jig* sing a rime   164
*Nestor* (the oldest and most reverend of the Greek chieftains)   *push-pin*
(a child's game)   165 *critic* cynic   *Timon* (Greek misanthrope)   *laugh . . .
toys* i.e. delight in useless trifles

Where lies thy grief? O, tell me, good Dumaine.
And, gentle Longaville, where lies thy pain?
And where my liege's? All about the breast.
A caudle, ho!

*King.*        Too bitter is thy jest.
Are we betrayed thus to thy over-view?      170

*Berowne.* Not you by me, but I betrayed to you;
I that am honest, I that hold it sin
To break the vow I am engagèd in,
I am betrayed by keeping company
With men like you, men of inconstancy.      175
When shall you see me write a thing in rime?
Or groan for Joan or spend a minute's time
In pruning me? When shall you hear that I
Will praise a hand, a foot, a face, an eye,
A gait, a state, a brow, a breast, a waist,      180
A leg, a limb —

*King.*        Soft! Whither away so fast?
A true man or a thief, that gallops so?

*Berowne.* I post from love. Good lover, let me go.

*Enter Jaquenetta and [Costard, the] Clown.*

*Jaquenetta.* God bless the king!
*King.*        What present hast thou there?
*Costard.* Some certain treason.
*King.*        What makes treason here?      185
*Costard.* Nay, it makes nothing, sir.
*King.*        If it mar nothing neither,
The treason and you go in peace away together.
*Jaquenetta.* I beseech your Grace let this letter be read:
Our parson misdoubts it; 'twas treason, he said.

169 *caudle* (warm liquid nourishment for the ill)   178 *pruning* trimming,
barbering   180 *state* bearing   185 *makes* does   189 *misdoubts* suspects

190  *King.* Berowne, read it over.

                              *He [Berowne] reads the letter.*

      Where hadst thou it?

*Jaquenetta.* Of Costard.

*King.* Where hadst thou it?

*Costard.* Of Dun Adramadio, Dun Adramadio.

                              *[Berowne tears the letter.]*

195  *King.* How now, what is in you? Why dost thou tear it?

*Berowne.* A toy, my liege, a toy. Your Grace needs not fear
      it.

*Longaville.* It did move him to passion, and therefore let's
      hear it.

*Dumaine. [picking up the pieces]* It is Berowne's writing, and
      here is his name.

*Berowne. [to Costard]* Ah, you whoreson loggerhead, you
      were born to do me shame.

200      Guilty, my lord, guilty. I confess, I confess.

*King.* What?

*Berowne.* That you three fools lacked me fool to make up
      the mess.

      He, he, and you — and you my liege, and I,

      Are pick-purses in love, and we deserve to die.

205  O dismiss this audience, and I shall tell you more.

*Dumaine.* Now the number is even.

*Berowne.*                              True, true; we are four.

      Will these turtles be gone?

*King.*                              Hence, sirs, away.

*Costard.* Walk aside the true folk, and let the traitors stay.

                              *[Exeunt Costard and Jaquenetta.]*

*Berowne.* Sweet lords, sweet lovers, O, let us embrace!

210      As true we are as flesh and blood can be;

196 *toy* trifle   199 *loggerhead* blockhead   202 *mess* (a group of four at
table)   204 *pick-purses* i.e. cheaters   207 *turtles* turtledoves, lovers

The sea will ebb and flow, heaven show his face:
Young blood doth not obey an old decree.
We cannot cross the cause why we were born;
Therefore, of all hands must we be forsworn.

*King.* What, did these rent lines show some love of thine? 215

*Berowne.* Did they? quoth you. Who sees the heavenly
   Rosaline,
That, like a rude and savage man of Inde,
At the first opening of the gorgeous east,
Bows not his vassal head and, strooken blind,
Kisses the base ground with obedient breast? 220
What peremptory eagle-sighted eye
Dares look upon the heaven of her brow,
That is not blinded by her majesty?

*King.* What zeal, what fury, hath inspired thee now?
My love, her mistress, is a gracious moon; 225
She, an attending star, scarce seen a light.

*Berowne.* My eyes are then no eyes, nor I Berowne.
O, but for my love, day would turn to night!
Of all complexions the culled sovereignty
Do meet, as at a fair, in her fair cheek, 230
Where several worthies make one dignity,
Where nothing wants that want itself doth seek.
Lend me the flourish of all gentle tongues —
Fie, painted rhetoric! O, she needs it not.
To things of sale a seller's praise belongs; 235
She passes praise; then praise too short doth blot.
A withered hermit, five-score winters worn,

213 *cross . . . born* combat the cause of our birth (love between the sexes)
214 *of all hands* in all events, inevitably  215 *rent lines* torn verses  217
*Inde* India  221 *peremptory* bold  229 *the culled sovereignty* those selected
as best  231 *several worthies* various excellences  232 *wants* lacks  *want*
desire  233 *flourish* adornment  234 *painted* artificial  235 *of sale* for
sale

Might shake off fifty, looking in her eye:
Beauty doth varnish age as if new-born,
240 And gives the crutch the cradle's infancy.
O, 'tis the sun that maketh all things shine!

*King.* By heaven, thy love is black as ebony.

*Berowne.* Is ebony like her? O wood divine!
A wife of such wood were felicity.
245 O, who can give an oath? Where is a book?
That I may swear beauty doth beauty lack,
If that she learn not of her eye to look.
No face is fair that is not full so black.

*King.* O paradox! Black is the badge of hell,
250 The hue of dungeons, and the school of night;
And beauty's crest becomes the heavens well.

*Berowne.* Devils soonest tempt, resembling spirits of light.
O, if in black my lady's brows be decked,
It mourns that painting and usurping hair
255 Should ravish doters with a false aspect;
And therefore is she born to make black fair.
Her favor turns the fashion of the days,
For native blood is counted painting now;
And therefore red that would avoid dispraise
260 Paints itself black to imitate her brow.

*Dumaine.* To look like her are chimney-sweepers black.

*Longaville.* And since her time are colliers counted bright.

*King.* And Ethiops of their sweet complexion crack.

*Dumaine.* Dark needs no candles now, for dark is light.

265 *Berowne.* Your mistresses dare never come in rain,
For fear their colors should be washed away.

245 *book* i.e. Bible   247 *of . . . look* i.e. from her (dark) eyes how to appear
250 *school* i.e. training place for evil night-work (?)   251 *And* and yet
*beauty's crest* i.e. blackness (according to Berowne's paradoxical conten-
tion)   252 *resembling* simulating   254 *usurping* false   257 *favor* face   258
*native blood* i.e. naturally red cheeks   *counted* accounted   263 *crack* boast

*King.* 'Twere good yours did; for, sir, to tell you plain,
  I'll find a fairer face not washed to-day.
*Berowne.* I'll prove her fair, or talk till doomsday here.
*King.* No devil will fright thee then so much as she.      270
*Dumaine.* I never knew man hold vile stuff so dear.
*Longaville.* Look, here's thy love — *[Shows his shoe.]* my
  foot and her face see.
*Berowne.* O, if the streets were pavèd with thine eyes,
  Her feet were much too dainty for such tread.
*Dumaine.* O vile! Then, as she goes, what upward lies      275
  The street should see as she walked overhead.
*King.* But what of this? Are we not all in love?
*Berowne.* O, nothing so sure, and thereby all forsworn.
*King.* Then leave this chat; and, good Berowne, now prove
  Our loving lawful and our faith not torn.      280
*Dumaine.* Ay, marry, there; some flattery for this evil.
*Longaville.* O some authority how to proceed;
  Some tricks, some quillets, how to cheat the devil.
*Dumaine.* Some salve for perjury.
*Berowne.*                              O, 'tis more than need.
  Have at you, then, affection's men-at-arms!      285
  Consider what you first did swear unto:
  To fast, to study, and to see no woman —
  Flat treason 'gainst the kingly state of youth.
  Say, can you fast? Your stomachs are too young,
  And abstinence engenders maladies.      290
  [And where that you have vowed to study, lords,
  In that each of you have forsworn his book,

268 *I'll . . . to-day* i.e. there are other unwashed faces fairer than hers
270 *then* i.e. on doomsday 281 *flattery* i.e. soothing lies 283 *quillets*
quibbles 285 *affection's men-at-arms* passion's followers 291–312 *And
where . . . learning there* (a passage probably marked for excision in the
manuscript, since another version follows) 291 *where that* whereas 292
*In that* inasmuch as *book* i.e. a woman's face

Can you still dream and pore and thereon look?
For when would you, my lord, or you, or you,
295   Have found the ground of study's excellence
Without the beauty of a woman's face?
From women's eyes this doctrine I derive:
They are the ground, the books, the academes,
From whence doth spring the true Promethean fire.
300   Why, universal plodding poisons up
The nimble spirits in the arteries,
As motion and long-during action tires
The sinewy vigor of the traveller.
Now, for not looking on a woman's face,
305   You have in that forsworn the use of eyes,
And study too, the causer of your vow;
For where is any author in the world
Teaches such beauty as a woman's eye?
Learning is but an adjunct to ourself,
310   And where we are our learning likewise is.
Then when ourselves we see in ladies' eyes,
Do we not likewise see our learning there?]
O, we have made a vow to study, lords,
And in that vow we have forsworn our books;
315   For when would you, my liege, or you, or you,
In leaden contemplation have found out
Such fiery numbers as the prompting eyes
Of beauty's tutors have enriched you with?
Other slow arts entirely keep the brain,
320   And therefore, finding barren practisers,
Scarce show a harvest of their heavy toil;
But love, first learnèd in a lady's eyes,

295 *ground* basis  298 *academes* academies  299 *Promethean* divine (the god
Prometheus brought fire from heaven to earth)  302 *long-during* enduring
317 *numbers* verses, poems  319 *arts* branches of knowledge  *keep* remain in

Lives not alone immurèd in the brain,
But, with the motion of all elements,
Courses as swift as thought in every power,                    325
And gives to every power a double power,
Above their functions and their offices.
It adds a precious seeing to the eye:
A lover's eyes will gaze an eagle blind.
A lover's ear will hear the lowest sound,                    330
When the suspicious head of theft is stopped.
Love's feeling is more soft and sensible
Than are the tender horns of cockled snails.
Love's tongue proves dainty Bacchus gross in taste.
For valor, is not Love a Hercules,                    335
Still climbing trees in the Hesperides?
Subtle as Sphinx; as sweet and musical
As bright Apollo's lute, strung with his hair.
And when Love speaks, the voice of all the gods
Make heaven drowsy with the harmony.                    340
Never durst poet touch a pen to write
Until his ink were temp'red with Love's sighs;
O, then his lines would ravish savage ears
And plant in tyrants mild humility.
From women's eyes this doctrine I derive.                    345
They sparkle still the right Promethean fire;
They are the books, the arts, the academes,
That show, contain, and nourish all the world;
Else none at all in aught proves excellent.
Then fools you were these women to forswear,                    350

324 *elements* (fire, air, water, earth, each of which had its own proper
motion and proper seat in the body as elsewhere)   327 *Above their functions* i.e. beyond their ordinary functions   331 *When . . . stopped* i.e. when
even a timorously alert thief hears nothing   332 *sensible* sensitive   333
*cockled* in shells   334 *Bacchus* (god of wine and feasting)   336 *Hesperides*
(where the golden apples grew)   342 *temp'red* cooled and refined

Or, keeping what is sworn, you will prove fools.
For wisdom's sake, a word that all men love,
Or for love's sake, a word that loves all men,
Or for men's sake, the authors of these women,
355   Or women's sake, by whom we men are men,
Let us once lose our oaths to find ourselves,
Or else we lose ourselves to keep our oaths.
It is religion to be thus forsworn,
For charity itself fulfils the law
360   And who can sever love from charity?

*King.* Saint Cupid then! And, soldiers, to the field!

*Berowne.* Advance your standards, and upon them, lords!
Pell-mell, down with them! But be first advised,
In conflict that you get the sun of them.

365 *Longaville.* Now to plain-dealing — lay these glozes by —
Shall we resolve to woo these girls of France?

*King.* And win them too; therefore let us devise
Some entertainment for them in their tents.

*Berowne.* First from the park let us conduct them thither;
370   Then homeward every man attach the hand
Of his fair mistress. In the afternoon
We will with some strange pastime solace them,
Such as the shortness of the time can shape;
For revels, dances, masks, and merry hours
375   Forerun fair Love, strewing her way with flowers.

*King.* Away, away! No time shall be omitted
That will be time, and may by us be fitted.

*Berowne.* Allons! allons! Sowed cockle reaped no corn;

351 *what is sworn* i.e. the oaths   353 *loves* i.e. is lovable to   356 *once* for once (?) at once (?)   359 *For . . . law* (Romans 13:8—'. . . for he that loveth another hath fulfilled the law')   364 *get . . . them* i.e. maneuver them into facing the sun (with play on 'beget son')   365 *glozes* sophistries 377 *be time* betime, come to pass   *fitted* utilized   378 *Allons* come   *cockle* a variety of weed   *corn* wheat

And justice always whirls in equal measure.
Light wenches may prove plagues to men forsworn;        380
If so, our copper buys no better treasure.        *[Exeunt.]*

*Enter [Holofernes,] the Pedant, [Nathaniel,] the Curate,*        V, i
*and Dull, [the Constable].*

*Holofernes.* Satis quid sufficit.

*Nathaniel.* I praise God for you, sir. Your reasons at dinner
have been sharp and sententious, pleasant without scurrility, witty without affection, audacious without im-
pudency, learned without opinion, and strange without 5
heresy. I did converse this quondam day with a compan-
ion of the king's, who is intituled, nominated, or called,
Don Adriano de Armado.

*Holofernes.* Novi hominem tanquam te. His humor is lofty,
his discourse peremptory, his tongue filed, his eye am- 10
bitious, his gait majestical, and his general behavior vain,
ridiculous, and thrasonical. He is too picked, too spruce,
too affected, too odd, as it were, too peregrinate, as I may
call it.

*Nathaniel.* A most singular and choice epithet.        15

*Draw out his table-book.*

*Holofernes.* He draweth out the thread of his verbosity finer

381 *copper* base coin (i.e. as men forsworn, they have little of worth to
offer)  V, i, 1 *Satis quid sufficit* (misquotation of 'satis est quod sufficit':
enough is as good as a feast)  2 *reasons* discourses  4 *affection* affectation
5 *opinion* self-conceit  *strange* novel  9 *Novi . . . te* I know the man as
well as I know you  10 *filed* smooth  12 *thrasonical* boastful  *picked*
finicking  13 *peregrinate* exotic  15 *singular* unique  15 S.D. *table-book*
tablet, notebook

than the staple of his argument. I abhor such fanatical
phantasimes, such insociable and point-devise companions; such rackers of orthography as to speak 'dout' fine
20    when he should say 'doubt'; 'det' when he should pronounce 'debt' — d, e, b, t, not d, e, t. He clepeth a calf
'cauf'; half 'hauf'; neighbor vocatur 'nebor,' neigh ab-
breviated 'ne.' This is abhominable, which he would call
'abominable.' It insinuateth me of insanie. Ne intelligis,
25    domine? To make frantic, lunatic.
*Nathaniel.* Laus Deo bone intelligo.
*Holofernes.* Bone? Bone for bene! Priscian a little scratched
— 'twill serve.

*Enter [Armado, the] Braggart, [Moth, the] Boy, [and
Costard, the Clown].*

*Nathaniel.* Videsne quis venit?
30 *Holofernes.* Video, et gaudeo.
*Armado. [to Moth]* Chirrah!
*Holofernes.* Quare 'chirrah,' not 'sirrah'?
*Armado.* Men of peace, well encountered.
*Holofernes.* Most military sir, salutation.
35 *Moth. [aside to Costard]* They have been at a great feast of
languages and stolen the scraps.
*Costard.* O, they have lived long on the alms-basket of
words. I marvel thy master hath not eaten thee for a

17 *staple* fibre   *argument* subject matter   18 *phantasimes* (cf. IV, i, 98)
*insociable* incompatible   18 *point-devise* precise   19 *fine* mincingly   21
*clepeth* calls   22 *vocatur* is called   24 *insanie* madness   24–25 *Ne . . . domine*
do you understand, sir   26 *Laus . . . intelligo* praise God, I understand well
27 *Priscian* i.e. Latin grammar (after the fifth-century grammarian whose
textbooks were long standard)   *scratched* marred   29 *Videsne quis venit* do
you see who comes   30 *Video, et gaudeo* I see and rejoice   32 *Quare* why
37 *alms-basket* container in which scraps for the poor were gathered

word; for thou art not so long by the head as honorificabilitudinitatibus. Thou art easier swallowed than a flap-   40
dragon.

*Moth.* Peace! The peal begins.

*Armado.* Monsieur, are you not lett'red?

*Moth.* Yes, yes! He teaches boys the horn-book. What is
a, b, spelled backward with the horn on his head?   45

*Holofernes.* Ba, pueritia, with a horn added.

*Moth.* Ba, most silly sheep with a horn. You hear his
learning.

*Holofernes.* Quis, quis, thou consonant?

*Moth.* The last of the five vowels, if you repeat them; or the   50
fifth, if I.

*Holofernes.* I will repeat them: a, e, i —

*Moth.* The sheep. The other two concludes it — o, u.

*Armado.* Now, by the salt wave of the Mediterranean, a
sweet touch, a quick venew of wit! Snip, snap, quick and   55
home! It rejoiceth my intellect. True wit!

*Moth.* Offered by a child to an old man — which is wit-old.

*Holofernes.* What is the figure? What is the figure?

*Moth.* Horns.

*Holofernes.* Thou disputes like an infant. Go whip thy gig.   60

*Moth.* Lend me your horn to make one, and I will whip
about your infamy manu cita. A gig of a cuckold's horn.

---

39–40 *honorificabilitudinitatibus* condition of being capable of honors
(given in the dative plural and often cited as the 'longest word' in exist-
ence)   40–41 *flap-dragon* a drink of brandy containing a burning raisin   42
*peal* i.e. clatter of tongues   43 *lett'red* i.e. a man of letters   44 *horn-book*
(printed sheets covered by transparent horn, for teaching the alphabet)
46 *pueritia* child   49 *Quis* what   *consonant* i.e. nonentity (because in pro-
nunciation the consonants require vowels)   53 *o, u* (oh you)   55 *venew*
venue, sally   57 *wit-old* i.e. wittol, tame cuckold   58 *figure* metaphor
60 *gig* top   62 *manu cita* with ready hand (the Latin is a conjectural emendation for the meaningless 'unum cita' of the quarto)

*Costard.* An I had but one penny in the world, thou shouldst
have it to buy gingerbread. Hold, there is the very re-
65  muneration I had of thy master, thou halfpenny purse of
wit, thou pigeon-egg of discretion. O, an the heavens
were so pleased that thou wert but my bastard, what a
joyful father wouldest thou make me! Go to, thou hast it
ad dunghill, at the fingers' ends, as they say.

70  *Holofernes.* O, I smell false Latin! 'Dunghill' for unguem.

*Armado.* Arts-man, preambulate. We will be singled from
the barbarous. Do you not educate youth at the charge-
house on the top of the mountain?

*Holofernes.* Or mons, the hill.

75  *Armado.* At your sweet pleasure, for the mountain.

*Holofernes.* I do, sans question.

*Armado.* Sir, it is the king's most sweet pleasure and affection to congratulate the princess at her pavilion in the
posteriors of this day, which the rude multitude call the
80  afternoon.

*Holofernes.* The posterior of the day, most generous sir, is
liable, congruent, and measurable for the afternoon. The
word is well culled, chose, sweet and apt, I do assure you,
sir, I do assure.

85  *Armado.* Sir, the king is a noble gentleman, and my familiar,
I do assure ye, very good friend. For what is inward between us, let it pass. I do beseech thee remember thy
courtesy. I beseech thee apparel thy head. And among

65 *halfpenny purse* (a novelty purse, just large enough to hold a halfpenny)
69 *ad dunghill* (malapropism for 'ad unguem,' i.e. on the nail)  71 *Arts-man* scholar  *preambulate* come  *singled* distinguished  72–73 *charge-house
.... mountain* (an obscure allusion, possibly involving an academic joke
about the kind of school mentioned in Erasmus's *Familiaria Colloquia*,
where the paying pupils acquired more lice than Latin)  81 *generous* culti-
vated  82 *liable* suitable  *congruent* appropriate  *measurable* meet  85
*familiar* intimate  86 *inward* private  87–88 *thy courtesy* i.e. that you have
removed your hat

other importunate and most serious designs, and of great
import indeed, too — but let that pass; for I must tell thee, 90
it will please his Grace, by the world, sometime to lean
upon my poor shoulder, and with his royal finger thus dally
with my excrement, with my mustachio — but, sweet
heart, let that pass. By the world, I recount no fable: some
certain special honors it pleaseth his greatness to impart to 95
Armado, a soldier, a man of travel, that hath seen the
world — but let that pass. The very all of all is (but, sweet
heart, I do implore secrecy) that the king would have me
present the princess, sweet chuck, with some delightful
ostentation, or show, or pageant, or antic, or fire-work. 100
Now, understanding that the curate and your sweet self
are good at such eruptions and sudden breaking out of
mirth, as it were, I have acquainted you withal, to the end
to crave your assistance.

*Holofernes.* Sir, you shall present before her the Nine 105
Worthies. Sir Nathaniel, as concerning some entertainment of time, some show in the posterior of this day, to be
rend'red by our assistance, the king's command, and this
most gallant, illustrate, and learned gentleman, before the
princess — I say, none so fit as to present the Nine 110
Worthies.

*Nathaniel.* Where will you find men worthy enough to present them?

*Holofernes.* Joshua, yourself; myself; and this gallant gentleman, Judas Maccabaeus; this swain, because of his great 115

93 *excrement* excrescence, hair   100 *antic* (a pageant or pantomime in
whimsical costume)   105–6 *Nine Worthies* (conquerors commonly fea-
tured in folk-drama and pageants: Hector, Alexander, Caesar, Joshua,
David, Judas Maccabaeus, King Arthur, Charlemagne, and Godfrey of
Bouillon or Guy of Warwick; in the present case Hercules and Pompey
are substituted for more usual figures)   114 *myself* (Holofernes does not
specify his own part, perhaps by a printer's error)

limb or joint, shall pass Pompey the Great; the page,
Hercules —

*Armado.* Pardon, sir — error. He is not quantity enough for
that Worthy's thumb; he is not so big as the end of his
120 club.

*Holofernes.* Shall I have audience? He shall present Hercules
in minority. His enter and exit shall be strangling a snake;
and I will have an apology for that purpose.

*Moth.* An excellent device! So if any of the audience hiss,
125 you may cry, 'Well done, Hercules! Now thou crushest
the snake!' That is the way to make an offense gracious,
though few have the grace to do it.

*Armado.* For the rest of the Worthies?

*Holofernes.* I will play three myself.

130 *Moth.* Thrice-worthy gentleman!

*Armado.* Shall I tell you a thing?

*Holofernes.* We attend.

*Armado.* We will have, if this fadge not, an antic. I beseech
you, follow.

135 *Holofernes.* Via, goodman Dull! Thou hast spoken no word
all this while.

*Dull.* Nor understood none neither, sir.

*Holofernes.* Allons! we will employ thee.

*Dull.* I'll make one in a dance, or so; or I will play on the
140 tabor to the Worthies, and let them dance the hay.

*Holofernes.* Most dull, honest Dull. To our sport, away!

*Exeunt.*

116 *pass* perform    121 *audience* a hearing    122 *snake* (the legendary
Hercules strangled in his cradle two snakes sent by Juno to destroy him)
123 *apology* explanation, justification    133 *fadge not* does not succeed
*antic* (cf. l. 100, above)    135 *Via* i.e. go on (a cry of encouragement)
138 *Allons* come    140 *tabor* small drum   *the hay* (country dance resembling a reel)

*Enter the Ladies [Princess, Katharine, Rosaline, and*    V, ii
    *Maria].*

*Princess.* Sweet hearts, we shall be rich ere we depart
    If fairings come thus plentifully in.
    A lady walled about with diamonds!
    Look you what I have from the loving king.
*Rosaline.* Madam, came nothing else along with that?    5
*Princess.* Nothing but this? Yes, as much love in rime
    As would be crammed up in a sheet of paper,
    Writ o' both sides the leaf, margent and all,
    That he was fain to seal on Cupid's name.
*Rosaline.* That was the way to make his godhead wax,    10
    For he hath been five thousand year a boy.
*Katharine.* Ay, and a shrewd unhappy gallows too.
*Rosaline.* You'll ne'er be friends with him: 'a killed your
    sister.
*Katharine.* He made her melancholy, sad, and heavy;
    And so she died. Had she been light, like you,    15
    Of such a merry, nimble, stirring spirit,
    She might ha' been a grandam ere she died;
    And so may you, for a light heart lives long.
*Rosaline.* What's your dark meaning, mouse, of this light
    word?
*Katharine.* A light condition in a beauty dark.    20
*Rosaline.* We need more light to find your meaning out.
*Katharine.* You'll mar the light by taking it in snuff;
    Therefore, I'll darkly end the argument.

V, ii, 2 *fairings* gifts, tokens bought at a fair  8 *margent* margin  9 *That
. . . name* i.e. so that he was willing in the circumstances to include Cupid's
name on an appended seal  10 *wax* grow (with play on wax seal)  12
*shrewd unhappy gallows* vexing mischievous knave  20 *light* wanton, wayward  22 *taking . . . snuff* i.e. being offended by it (with play on snuffing
a candle)  23 *darkly* without clarifying (?)

*Rosaline.* Look, what you do, you do it still i' th' dark.

25 *Katharine.* So do not you, for you are a light wench.

*Rosaline.* Indeed I weigh not you, and therefore light.

*Katharine.* You weigh me not? O! that's you care not for
  me.

*Rosaline.* Great reason; for past cure is still past care.

*Princess.* Well bandied both, a set of wit well played.

30   But, Rosaline, you have a favor too:
  Who sent it? and what is it?

*Rosaline.*                     I would you knew.
  An if my face were but as fair as yours,
  My favor were as great. Be witness this.
  Nay, I have verses too, I thank Berowne:

35   The numbers true; and, were the numb'ring too,
  I were the fairest goddess on the ground.
  I am compared to twenty thousand fairs.
  O, he hath drawn my picture in his letter!

*Princess.* Anything like?

40 *Rosaline.* Much in the letters, nothing in the praise.

*Princess.* Beauteous as ink — a good conclusion.

*Katharine.* Fair as a text B in a copy-book.

*Rosaline.* 'Ware pencils, ho! Let me not die your debtor,
  My red dominical, my golden letter.

45   O, that your face were not so full of O's!

*Princess.* A pox of that jest, and I beshrew all shrows!
  But, Katharine, what was sent to you from fair Dumaine?

---

26 *weigh* (1) equal in weight (2) regard  28 *past cure* (Rosaline is calling
Katharine 'incurable')  29 *bandied* volleyed  30 *favor* gift  35 *numbers*
meter  *numb'ring* reckoning  37 *fairs* fair women  40 *letters . . . praise* i.e.
in the orthography rather than in the content (?)  42 *a text B* (a capital
printed in Gothic text or 'black-letter'; the allusion is to Rosaline's dark
complexion)  43 *'Ware pencils* i.e. have at you (with the metaphor still
drawn from the arts of writing and portraiture)  44 *red dominical* the red letters used to mark Sundays and holy days in almanacs, etc. (the allusion seems
to be to Katharine's ruddy pock-marks)  46 *beshrew all shrows* curse all scolds

*Katharine.* Madam, this glove.
*Princess.*                    Did he not send you twain?
*Katharine.* Yes, madam; and moreover,
  Some thousand verses of a faithful lover:                    50
  A huge translation of hypocrisy,
  Vilely compiled, profound simplicity.
*Maria.* This, and these pearls, to me sent Longaville.
  The letter is too long by half a mile.
*Princess.* I think no less. Dost thou not wish in heart                    55
  The chain were longer and the letter short?
*Maria.* Ay, or I would these hands might never part.
*Princess.* We are wise girls to mock our lovers so.
*Rosaline.* They are worse fools to purchase mocking so.
  That same Berowne I'll torture ere I go.                    60
  O that I knew he were but in by th' week!
  How I would make him fawn, and beg, and seek,
  And wait the season, and observe the times,
  And spend his prodigal wits in bootless rimes,
  And shape his service wholly to my hests,                    65
  And make him proud to make me proud that jests!
  So pertaunt-like would I o'ersway his state
  That he should be my fool, and I his fate.
*Princess.* None are so surely caught, when they are catched,
  As wit turned fool. Folly, in wisdom hatched,                    70
  Hath wisdom's warrant and the help of school
  And wit's own grace to grace a learnèd fool.
*Rosaline.* The blood of youth burns not with such excess
  As gravity's revolt to wantonness.
*Maria.* Folly in fools bears not so strong a note                    75

51 *translation* i.e. rendition  52 *simplicity* stupidity  59 *purchase* i.e. bid for, invite  61 *in . . . week* permanently caught  65 *hests* behests, commands  66 *proud to . . . jests* i.e. take pride in being the victim of my mockery (?)  67 *pertaunt* pair-taunt (winning hand in a card game called 'post and pair')  68 *fool* plaything

As fool'ry in the wise when wit doth dote;
Since all the power thereof it doth apply
To prove, by wit, worth in simplicity.


*Enter Boyet.*


*Princess.* Here comes Boyet, and mirth is in his face.
80  *Boyet.* O, I am stabbed with laughter! Where's her Grace?
*Princess.* Thy news, Boyet?
*Boyet.*                    Prepare, madam, prepare!
Arm, wenches, arm! Encounters mounted are
Against your peace. Love doth approach disguised,
Armèd in arguments; you'll be surprised.
85  Muster your wits; stand in your own defense,
Or hide your heads like cowards, and fly hence.
*Princess.* Saint Denis to Saint Cupid! What are they
That charge their breath against us? Say, scout, say.
*Boyet.* Under the cool shade of a sycamore
90  I thought to close mine eyes some half an hour,
When, lo, to interrupt my purposed rest,
Toward that shade I might behold addrest
The king and his companions! Warily
I stole into a neighbor thicket by,
95  And overheard what you shall overhear —
That, by and by, disguised they will be here.
Their herald is a pretty knavish page,
That well by heart hath conned his embassage.
Action and accent did they teach him there:
100  'Thus must thou speak, and thus thy body bear.'
And ever and anon they made a doubt

76 *dote* grow foolish  84 *surprised* i.e. overcome by surprise attack  87
*Saint Denis* (patron saint of France)  92 *addrest* marching  98 *embassage*
message of state  99 *Action* gesture  101 *made a doubt* expressed a fear

Presence majestical would put him out;
'For,' quoth the king, 'an angel shalt thou see;
Yet fear not thou, but speak audaciously.'
The boy replied, 'An angel is not evil;     105
I should have feared her had she been a devil.'
With that all laughed and clapped him on the shoulder,
Making the bold wag by their praises bolder.
One rubbed his elbow thus, and fleered, and swore
A better speech was never spoke before.     110
Another, with his finger and his thumb,
Cried 'Via, we will do 't, come what will come!'
The third he capered and cried, 'All goes well!'
The fourth turned on the toe, and down he fell.
With that they all did tumble on the ground     115
With such a zealous laughter, so profound,
That in this spleen ridiculous appears,
To check their folly, passion's solemn tears.

*Princess.* But what, but what? Come they to visit us?

*Boyet.* They do, they do; and are apparelled thus,     120
Like Muscovites or Russians, as I guess.
Their purpose is to parle, to court and dance;
And every one his love-feat will advance
Unto his several mistress, which they'll know
By favors several which they did bestow.     125

*Princess.* And will they so? The gallants shall be tasked:
For, ladies, we will every one be masked,
And not a man of them shall have the grace,
Despite of suit, to see a lady's face.
Hold, Rosaline, this favor thou shalt wear,     130

104 *audaciously* boldly  109 *fleered* grinned  111 *with ... thumb* i.e. with a snapping of the fingers  112 *Via* go on  116 *profound* deep  117 *spleen ridiculous* fit of laughing  122 *parle* parley  123 *love-feat* display of prowess in courtship  124 *which* whom  126 *tasked* hard put to it  128 *grace* favor  129 *Despite of suit* in spite of his plea

And then the king will court thee for his dear:
Hold, take thou this, my sweet, and give me thine;
So shall Berowne take me for Rosaline.
And change you favors too; so shall your loves
135     Woo contrary, deceived by these removes.
*Rosaline.* Come on, then — wear the favors most in sight.
*Katharine.* But in this changing what is your intent?
*Princess.* The effect of my intent is to cross theirs.
They do it but in mockery merriment,
140     And mock for mock is only my intent.
Their several counsels they unbosom shall
To loves mistook and so be mocked withal
Upon the next occasion that we meet,
With visages displayed, to talk and greet.
145 *Rosaline.* But shall we dance if they desire us to 't?
*Princess.* No, to the death we will not move a foot,
Nor to their penned speech render we no grace,
But while 'tis spoke each turn away her face.
*Boyet.* Why, that contempt will kill the speaker's heart,
150     And quite divorce his memory from his part.
*Princess.* Therefore I do it, and I make no doubt
The rest will ne'er come in if he be out.
There's no such sport as sport by sport o'erthrown,
To make theirs ours, and ours none but our own.
155     So shall we stay, mocking intended game,
And they, well mocked, depart away with shame.
                                        *Sound Trumpets.*
*Boyet.* The trumpet sounds. Be masked. The maskers come.
                                *[ The Ladies mask. ]*

---

135 *removes* exchanges   136 *most in sight* conspicuously   139 *mockery*
mocking   141 *several* individual   *unbosom* confide   146 *No . . . death* i.e.
not on your life   154 *theirs* i.e. their sport   155 *game* i.e. mockery

*Enter Blackamoors with music; [Moth,] the Boy, with a*
*speech, and the rest of the Lords disguised.*

*Moth.* 'All hail, the richest beauties on the earth!'
*Boyet.* Beauties no richer than rich taffeta.
*Moth.* 'A holy parcel of the fairest dames,                    160
                    *The Ladies turn their backs to him.*
     That ever turned their – backs – to mortal views!'
*Berowne.* 'Their eyes,' villain, 'their eyes.'
*Moth.* 'That ever turned their eyes to mortal views!
     Out –'
*Boyet.* True. 'Out' indeed.                                    165
*Moth.* 'Out of your favors, heavenly spirits, vouchsafe
     Not to behold' –
*Berowne.* 'Once to behold,' rogue.
*Moth.* 'Once to behold with your sun-beamèd eyes,
     – with your sun-beamèd eyes' –                             170
*Boyet.* They will not answer to that epithet.
     You were best call it 'daughter-beamèd eyes.'
*Moth.* They do not mark me, and that brings me out.
*Berowne.* Is this your perfectness? Be gone, you rogue!
                                        *[Exit Moth.]*
*Rosaline.* What would these strangers? Know their minds,
     Boyet.                                                     175
     If they do speak our language, 'tis our will
     That some plain man recount their purposes.
     Know what they would.
*Boyet.* What would you with the Princess?
*Berowne.* Nothing but peace and gentle visitation.            180
*Rosaline.* What would they, say they?

159 *taffeta* i.e. the cloth of their masks   165 *Out* i.e. out of his part   172
*daughter* (the inevitable play on 'sun-son')

*Boyet.* Nothing but peace and gentle visitation.

*Rosaline.* Why, that they have, and bid them so be
    gone.

*Boyet.* She says you have it and you may be gone.

185 *King.* Say to her, we have measured many miles,
    To tread a measure with her on this grass.

*Boyet.* They say that they have measured many a mile,
    To tread a measure with you on this grass.

*Rosaline.* It is not so. Ask them how many inches
190   Is in one mile. If they have measured many,
    The measure then of one is easily told.

*Boyet.* If to come hither you have measured miles,
    And many miles, the princess bids you tell
    How many inches doth fill up one mile.

195 *Berowne.* Tell her we measure them by weary steps.

*Boyet.* She hears herself.

*Rosaline.*                How many weary steps,
    Of many weary miles you have o'ergone,
    Are numb'red in the travel of one mile?

*Berowne.* We number nothing that we spend for you.
200   Our duty is so rich, so infinite,
    That we may do it still without accompt.
    Vouchsafe to show the sunshine of your face,
    That we, like savages, may worship it.

*Rosaline.* My face is but a moon, and clouded too.

205 *King.* Blessèd are clouds, to do as such clouds do.
    Vouchsafe, bright moon, and these thy stars, to shine
    (Those clouds removed) upon our watery eyne.

*Rosaline.* O vain petitioner, beg a greater matter!
    Thou now requests but moonshine in the water.

---

185 *measured* paced  186 *measure* dance  201 *accompt* accounting  207 *eyne*
eyes  209 *moonshine . . . water* i.e. nothing at all

*King.* Then in our measure do but vouchsafe one change. 210
  Thou bid'st me beg; this begging is not strange.
*Rosaline.* Play, music then. Nay, you must do it soon.
                              *[Music plays.]*
  Not yet — no dance! Thus change I like the moon.
*King.* Will you not dance? How come you thus estrangèd?
*Rosaline.* You took the moon at full, but now she's
    changèd.                                        215
*King.* Yet still she is the moon, and I the man.
  The music plays; vouchsafe some motion to it.
*Rosaline.* Our ears vouchsafe it.
*King.*                          But your legs should do it.
*Rosaline.* Since you are strangers and come here by chance,
  We'll not be nice: take hands — we will not dance. 220
*King.* Why take we hands then?
*Rosaline.*                      Only to part friends.
  Curtsy, sweet hearts; and so the measure ends.
*King.* More measure of this measure! Be not nice.
*Rosaline.* We can afford no more at such a price.
*King.* Price you yourselves. What buys your company?  225
*Rosaline.* Your absence only.
*King.*                        That can never be.
*Rosaline.* Then cannot we be bought; and so adieu —
  Twice to your visor, and half once to you.
*King.* If you deny to dance, let's hold more chat.
*Rosaline.* In private then.
*King.*                      I am best pleased with that.  230
                              *[They converse apart.]*

210 *change* round in a dance (with play on 'change of the moon') 211 *not strange* not foreign (even though begged by 'Muscovites') 213 *Not . . . dance* (she abruptly revokes her consent) 216 *man* i.e. man in the moon 217 *motion* response 220 *nice* coy 223 *More measure* i.e. a greater quantity 228 *visor* mask

*Berowne.* White-handed mistress, one sweet word with
 thee.
*Princess.* Honey, and milk, and sugar — there is three.
*Berowne.* Nay then, two treys, an if you grow so nice,
 Metheglin, wort, and malmsey — well run, dice!
 There's half a dozen sweets.
235 *Princess.*                     Seventh sweet, adieu.
 Since you can cog, I'll play no more with you.
*Berowne.* One word in secret.
*Princess.*                     Let it not be sweet.
*Berowne.* Thou grievest my gall.
*Princess.*                     Gall! Bitter.
*Berowne.*                              Therefore meet.
                              *[They converse apart.]*
*Dumaine.* Will you vouchsafe with me to change a word?
*Maria.* Name it.
*Dumaine.*           Fair lady —
240 *Maria.*                     Say you so? Fair lord.
 Take that for your 'fair lady.'
*Dumaine.*                     Please it you,
 As much in private, and I'll bid adieu.
                              *[They converse apart.]*
*Katharine.* What, was your vizard made without a tongue?
*Longaville.* I know the reason, lady, why you ask.
245 *Katharine.* O for your reason! Quickly, sir; I long.
*Longaville.* You have a double tongue within your mask
 And would afford my speechless vizard half.
*Katharine.* 'Veal,' quoth the Dutchman. Is not 'veal' a calf?
*Longaville.* A calf, fair lady?

233 *two treys* i.e. I'll double your 'trey' with three more words  *an if* if
234 *Metheglin* Welsh drink brewed from honey  *wort* unfermented or
'sweet' beer  *malmsey* sweet wine  236 *cog* cheat  238 *meet* appropriate
243 *vizard* mask  248 *Veal* i.e. 'well' in Dutch dialect (with play on 'veil'
—the vizard—as well as 'veal'—calf)

*Katharine.*             No, a fair lord calf.

*Longaville.* Let's part the word.

*Katharine.*          No, I'll not be your half:    250
   Take all and wean it — it may prove an ox.

*Longaville.* Look how you butt yourself in these sharp
     mocks.
   Will you give horns, chaste lady? Do not so.

*Katharine.* Then die a calf before your horns do grow.

*Longaville.* One word in private with you ere I die.    255

*Katharine.* Bleat softly then. The butcher hears you cry.
                       *[They converse apart.]*

*Boyet.* The tongues of mocking wenches are as keen
   As is the razor's edge invisible,
   Cutting a smaller hair than may be seen;
   Above the sense of sense, so sensible    260
   Seemeth their conference, their conceits have wings
   Fleeter than arrows, bullets, wind, thought, swifter
     things.

*Rosaline.* Not one word more, my maids! Break off, break
   off.

*Berowne.* By heaven, all dry-beaten with pure scoff!

*King.* Farewell, mad wenches. You have simple wits.    265
                   *Exeunt [King and Lords].*

*Princess.* Twenty adieus, my frozen Muscovits.
   Are these the breed of wits so wondered at?

*Boyet.* Tapers they are, with your sweet breaths puffed out.

*Rosaline.* Well-liking wits they have; gross, gross; fat, fat.

*Princess.* O poverty in wit, kingly-poor flout!    270

251 *wean* i.e. raise   252 *butt* i.e. injure, cast aspersions upon   253 *give horns* i.e. prove an unfaithful wife   260 *sense of* i.e. reach of   *sensible* nimble-witted   261 *conference* conversation    *conceits* fancies   264 *dry-beaten* clubbed, bruised   269 *Well-liking* ready for market, fat (as in 'fat-headed') 270 *kingly-poor* (a play on preceding 'liking'—i.e. like king, king-like, kingly)

Will they not, think you, hang themselves to-night?
Or ever but in vizards show their faces?
This pert Berowne was out of count'nance quite.
*Rosaline.* They were all in lamentable cases.
275  The king was weeping-ripe for a good word.
*Princess.* Berowne did swear himself out of all suit.
*Maria.* Dumaine was at my service, and his sword:
     'No point,' quoth I; my servant straight was mute.
*Katharine.* Lord Longaville said I came o'er his heart;
     And trow you what he called me?
280 *Princess.*                              Qualm, perhaps.
*Katharine.* Yes, in good faith.
*Princess.*                         Go, sickness as thou art!
*Rosaline.* Well, better wits have worn plain statute-caps.
     But will you hear? The king is my love sworn.
*Princess.* And quick Berowne hath plighted faith to me.
285 *Katharine.* And Longaville was for my service born.
*Maria.* Dumaine is mine as sure as bark on tree.
*Boyet.* Madam, and pretty mistresses, give ear.
     Immediately they will again be here
     In their own shapes, for it can never be
290  They will digest this harsh indignity.
*Princess.* Will they return?
*Boyet.*                        They will, they will, God knows,
     And leap for joy though they are lame with blows.
     Therefore change favors, and when they repair,
     Blow like sweet roses in this summer air.
295 *Princess.* How blow? how blow? Speak to be understood.

275 *weeping-ripe* i.e. ready to cry  276 *out . . . suit* (1) excessively (2) un-
availingly  278 *No point* (cf. II, i, 188)  280 *trow you* would you believe
281 *Go, sickness* (a play on 'qualm'—pronounced 'come'—in the preceding
line)  282 *Well . . . statute-caps* i.e. there have been cleverer people among
ordinary citizens (whose head-dress was regulated by statute)  293 *change
favors* exchange tokens  *repair* i.e. repair hither, arrive

*Boyet.* Fair ladies, masked, are roses in their bud;
   Dismasked, their damask sweet commixture shown,
   Are angels vailing clouds, or roses blown.
*Princess.* Avaunt, perplexity! What shall we do
   If they return in their own shapes to woo?     300
*Rosaline.* Good madam, if by me you'll be advised,
   Let's mock them still, as well known as disguised.
   Let us complain to them what fools were here,
   Disguised like Muscovites in shapeless gear;
   And wonder what they were, and to what end     305
   Their shallow shows and prologue vilely penned,
   And their rough carriage so ridiculous,
   Should be presented at our tent to us.
*Boyet.* Ladies, withdraw. The gallants are at hand.
*Princess.* Whip to your tents, as roes run o'er the land.     310

                  *Exeunt [Princess and Ladies].*

      *Enter the King and the rest [the Lords].*

*King.* Fair sir, God save you. Where's the Princess?
*Boyet.* Gone to her tent. Please it your Majesty
   Command me any service to her thither?
*King.* That she vouchsafe me audience for one word.
*Boyet.* I will; and so will she, I know, my lord.     *Exit.* 315
*Berowne.* This fellow pecks up wit, as pigeons pease,
   And utters it again when God doth please.
   He is wit's pedlar, and retails his wares
   At wakes and wassails, meetings, markets, fairs;
   And we that sell by gross, the Lord doth know,     320
   Have not the grace to grace it with such show.

---

297 *damask* i.e. mingled red and white complexion   298 *vailing* shedding
*blown* i.e. full-blown   299 *Avaunt, perplexity* i.e. away with riddling
317 *utters* issues, vends   319 *wakes* night revels   *wassails* drinking
sessions   320 *by gross* wholesale

This gallant pins the wenches on his sleeve.
Had he been Adam, he had tempted Eve.
'A can carve too, and lisp. Why, this is he
325   That kissed his hand away in courtesy.
This is the ape of form, monsieur the nice,
That, when he plays at tables, chides the dice
In honorable terms. Nay, he can sing
A mean most meanly; and in ushering
330   Mend him who can. The ladies call him sweet.
The stairs, as he treads on them, kiss his feet.
This is the flow'r that smiles on every one,
To show his teeth as white as whalës-bone;
And consciences that will not die in debt
335   Pay him the due of 'honey-tongued Boyet.'
*King.* A blister on his sweet tongue, with my heart,
That put Armado's page out of his part!

*Enter the Ladies [with Boyet].*

*Berowne.* See where it comes! Behavior, what wert thou,
Till this madman showed thee? and what art thou now?
340   *King.* All hail, sweet madam, and fair time of day.
*Princess.* 'Fair' in 'all hail' is foul, as I conceive.
*King.* Construe my speeches better, if you may.
*Princess.* Then wish me better — I will give you leave.
*King.* We came to visit you, and purpose now
345   To lead you to our court. Vouchsafe it then.
*Princess.* This field shall hold me, and so hold your vow.
Nor God nor I delights in perjured men.

---

324 *carve* i.e. woo by flattery  326 *nice* foppish  327 *tables* i.e. backgam-
mon  329 *mean* (an 'in-between' vocal part)  *ushering* i.e. playing the
groom or gentleman-in-waiting  338 *Behavior* i.e. fine manners  339
*madman* wag, madcap  341 *all . . . foul* i.e. a fall of hail means foul weather
346 *so hold* so uphold

*King.* Rebuke me not for that which you provoke.
  The virtue of your eye must break my oath.
*Princess.* You nickname virtue. 'Vice' you should have
    spoke;                                                                    350
  For virtue's office never breaks men's troth.
  Now, by my maiden honor, yet as pure
  As the unsullied lily, I protest,
  A world of torments though I should endure,
  I would not yield to be your house's guest,                        355
  So much I hate a breaking cause to be
  Of heavenly oaths, vowed with integrity.
*King.* O, you have lived in desolation here,
  Unseen, unvisited, much to our shame.
*Princess.* Not so, my lord. It is not so, I swear.           360
  We have had pastimes here and pleasant game.
  A mess of Russians left us but of late.
*King.* How, madam? Russians?
*Princess.*                                   Ay, in truth, my lord;
  Trim gallants, full of courtship and of state.
*Rosaline.* Madam, speak true. It is not so, my lord.        365
  My lady, to the manner of the days,
  In courtesy gives undeserving praise.
  We four indeed confronted were with four
  In Russian habit. Here they stayed an hour
  And talked apace; and in that hour, my lord,                370
  They did not bless us with one happy word.
  I dare not call them fools; but this I think,
  When they are thirsty, fools would fain have drink.
*Berowne.* This jest is dry to me. Gentle sweet,

349 *virtue* power (with quibble following)  350 *nickname* miscall  356 *breaking cause* i.e. cause of breaking  362 *mess* group of four  366 *to* in  371
*happy* apt  374 *dry* tart

375  Your wit makes wise things foolish. When we greet
     With eyes best seeing heaven's fiery eye,
     By light we lose light. Your capacity
     Is of that nature that to your huge store
     Wise things seem foolish and rich things but poor.
380  *Rosaline.* This proves you wise and rich, for in my eye —
     *Berowne.* I am a fool and full of poverty.
     *Rosaline.* But that you take what doth to you belong,
     It were a fault to snatch words from my tongue.
     *Berowne.* O, I am yours, and all that I possess.
     *Rosaline.* All the fool mine?
385  *Berowne.*                    I cannot give you less.
     *Rosaline.* Which of the vizards was it that you wore?
     *Berowne.* Where? when? what vizard? Why demand you
          this?
     *Rosaline.* There, then, that vizard; that superfluous case
     That hid the worse, and showed the better face.
     *King.* We were descried. They'll mock us now down-
390       right.
     *Dumaine.* Let us confess, and turn it to a jest.
     *Princess.* Amazed, my lord? Why looks your Highness sad?
     *Rosaline.* Help! Hold his brows! He'll sound. Why look
          you pale?
     Seasick, I think, coming from Muscovy.
395  *Berowne.* Thus pour the stars down plagues for perjury.
     Can any face of brass hold longer out?
     Here stand I, lady; dart thy skill at me.
     Bruise me with scorn, confound me with a flout,
     Thrust thy sharp wit quite through my ignorance,

375 *your wit* i.e. the greatness of your wit   *foolish* i.e. seem foolish in
comparison   375–77 *When . . . lose light* i.e. the power of the sun dims
even the keenest sight   388 *case* covering   392 *Amazed* confused   393
*sound* swoon

Cut me to pieces with thy keen conceit; 400
And I will wish thee never more to dance,
Nor never more in Russian habit wait.
O, never will I trust to speeches penned,
Nor to the motion of a schoolboy's tongue,
Nor never come in vizard to my friend, 405
Nor woo in rime, like a blind harper's song.
Taffeta phrases, silken terms precise,
Three-piled hyperboles, spruce affection,
Figures pedantical — these summer flies
Have blown me full of maggot ostentation. 410
I do forswear them; and I here protest
By this white glove (how white the hand, God knows)
Henceforth my wooing mind shall be expressed
In russet yeas and honest kersey noes.
And to begin, wench — so God help me, law! — 415
My love to thee is sound, sans crack or flaw.

*Rosaline.* Sans 'sans,' I pray you.

*Berowne.* Yet I have a trick
Of the old rage. Bear with me, I am sick.
I'll leave it by degrees. Soft, let us see —
Write 'Lord have mercy on us' on those three. 420
They are infected, in their hearts it lies;
They have the plague, and caught it of your eyes.
These lords are visited; you are not free,
For the Lord's tokens on you do I see.

400 *conceit* fancy, ingenuity 401 *wish* invite 402 *wait* attend 405 *friend* sweetheart 406 *blind harper's* i.e. performing beggar's, street-singer's 407 *precise* i.e. finely discriminated, as in word-splitting 408 *Three-piled* deep-piled (as in richest velvet) *spruce affection* jaunty affectation 409 *Figures* figures of speech 410 *blown* laid eggs on 414 *russet* home-spun *kersey* woolen cloth 415 *law* (a 'homespun' expletive) 416 *sans* without 417 *Yet* still *trick* trace 418 *rage* fever 420 *Lord . . . us* (the words posted on houses containing victims of the plague) 423 *visited* infected *free* i.e. free of infection 424 *tokens* plague-spots

425 *Princess.* No, they are free that gave these tokens to us.

*Berowne.* Our states are forfeit. Seek not to undo us.

*Rosaline.* It is not so, for how can this be true,
That you stand forfeit, being those that sue?

*Berowne.* Peace! for I will not have to do with you.

430 *Rosaline.* Nor shall not if I do as I intend.

*Berowne.* Speak for yourselves. My wit is at an end.

*King.* Teach us, sweet madam, for our rude transgression
Some fair excuse.

*Princess.*                The fairest is confession.
Were you not here but even now disguised?

*King.* Madam, I was.

435 *Princess.*                And were you well advised?

*King.* I was, fair madam.

*Princess.*                When you then were here,
What did you whisper in your lady's ear?

*King.* That more than all the world I did respect her.

*Princess.* When she shall challenge this, you will reject her.

*King.* Upon mine honor, no.

440 *Princess.*                Peace, peace, forbear!
Your oath once broke, you force not to forswear.

*King.* Despise me when I break this oath of mine.

*Princess.* I will, and therefore keep it. Rosaline,
What did the Russian whisper in your ear?

445 *Rosaline.* Madam, he swore that he did hold me dear
As precious eyesight, and did value me
Above this world; adding thereto, moreover,
That he would wed me or else die my lover.

---

425 *free* i.e. liberal (with 'tokens' taken up in the sense of 'gifts')  426
*states* estates  *forfeit* subject to confiscation  *undo* i.e. free, absolve (continuing the play on the word 'free')  428 *sue* (i.e. instead of the ones sued)
435 *well advised* rational  441 *force . . . forswear* i.e. forswear without
effort

*Princess.* God give thee joy of him. The noble lord
    Most honorably doth uphold his word.                    450
*King.* What mean you, madam? By my life, my troth,
    I never swore this lady such an oath.
*Rosaline.* By heaven you did, and to confirm it plain
    You gave me this, but take it, sir, again.
*King.* My faith and this the Princess I did give.          455
    I knew her by this jewel on her sleeve.
*Princess.* Pardon me, sir, this jewel did she wear,
    And Lord Berowne, I thank him, is my dear.
    What, will you have me, or your pearl again?
*Berowne.* Neither of either; I remit both twain.           460
    I see the trick on 't. Here was a consent,
    Knowing aforehand of our merriment,
    To dash it like a Christmas comedy.
    Some carry-tale, some please-man, some slight zany,
    Some mumble-news, some trencher-knight, some Dick    465
    That smiles his cheek in years, and knows the trick
    To make my lady laugh when she's disposed,
    Told our intents before; which once disclosed,
    The ladies did change favors, and then we,
    Following the signs, wooed but the sign of she.        470
    Now, to our perjury to add more terror,
    We are again forsworn, in will and error.
    Much upon this 'tis. *[to Boyet]* And might not you
    Forestall our sport, to make us thus untrue?
    Do not you know my lady's foot by th' squier,          475

---

454 *this* i.e. the favor originally given the Princess  461 *consent* agreement
463 *like* i.e. as one does  464 *please-man* toady  *zany* stooge  465 *mumble-
news* gossip  *trencher-knight* parasite  466 *in years* i.e. into the wrinkles of
old age  470 *she* i.e. the mistress intended  473 *Much . . . 'tis* i.e. this is
about the way of it  475 *squier* square (i.e. have her measure, know how
to please her)

And laugh upon the apple of her eye?
And stand between her back, sir, and the fire,
Holding a trencher, jesting merrily?
You put our page out. Go, you are allowed.
480  Die when you will, a smock shall be your shroud.
You leer upon me, do you? There's an eye
Wounds like a leaden sword.
*Boyet.*                              Full merrily
Hath this brave manage, this career, been run.
*Berowne.*  Lo, he is tilting straight. Peace! I have done.

*Enter [Costard, the] Clown.*

485  Welcome, pure wit! Thou part'st a fair fray.
*Costard.*  O Lord, sir, they would know
Whether the three Worthies shall come in or no.
*Berowne.*  What, are there but three?
*Costard.*                              No, sir; but it is vara fine,
For every one pursents three.
*Berowne.*                    And three times thrice is nine.
490  *Costard.*  Not so, sir, under correction, sir, I hope, it is not so.
You cannot beg us, sir, I can assure you, sir; we know
what we know:
I hope, sir, three times thrice, sir —
*Berowne.*                              Is not nine?
*Costard.*  Under correction, sir, we know whereuntil it doth
amount.

---

476 *apple* pupil (i.e. keep your pleasantries a center of her attention)  478
*trencher* plate  479 *out* out of his part  *allowed* i.e. a privileged fool or
jester  480 *smock* petticoat  483 *manage* maneuver on horseback  *career*
gallop  484 *tilting straight* i.e. at his word-play immediately  485 *pure
wit* i.e. Costard (as compared to Boyet)  491 *beg us* prove us fools (derived from the practice of seeking administration of the property of
mental defectives)

*Berowne.* By Jove, I always took three threes for nine.        495

*Costard.* O Lord, sir, it were pity you should get your living
  by reck'ning, sir.

*Berowne.* How much is it?

*Costard.* O Lord, sir, the parties themselves, the actors, sir,
  will show whereuntil it doth amount. For mine own    500
  part, I am, as they say, but to parfect one man in one poor
  man — Pompion the Great, sir.

*Berowne.* Art thou one of the Worthies?

*Costard.* It pleased them to think me worthy of Pompey the
  Great. For mine own part, I know not the degree of the    505
  Worthy, but I am to stand for him.

*Berowne.* Go, bid them prepare.

*Costard.* We will turn it finely off, sir; we will take some
  care.                                            *Exit.*

*King.* Berowne, they will shame us. Let them not approach.

*Berowne.* We are shame-proof, my lord; and 'tis some
  policy                                            510
  To have one show worse than the king's and his company.

*King.* I say they shall not come.

*Princess.* Nay, my good lord, let me o'errule you now.
  That sport best pleases that doth least know how;
  Where zeal strives to content, and the contents    515
  Dies in the zeal of that which it presents.
  Their form confounded makes most form in mirth
  When great things laboring perish in their birth.

*Berowne.* A right description of our sport, my lord.

496 *pity* i.e. too bad if  501 *parfect* perform (malapropism)  502 *Pompion*
pumpkin  510 *policy* good policy  515 *contents* substance  516 *of that . . .
presents* i.e. of the performance which presents this substance  517 *form
confounded* i.e. ruined artistry  *most form* i.e. superior artistry  519 *right*
exact  *our sport* i.e. our show of Muscovites

*Enter [Armado, the] Braggart.*

520 *Armado.* Anointed, I implore so much expense of thy
      royal sweet breath as will utter a brace of words.
         *[Converses with the King, and delivers a paper to him.]*
      *Princess.* Doth this man serve God?
      *Berowne.* Why ask you?
      *Princess.* 'A speaks not like a man of God his making.
525 *Armado.* That is all one, my fair, sweet, honey monarch;
      for, I protest, the schoolmaster is exceeding fantastical —
      too-too vain, too-too vain — but we will put it, as they
      say, to fortuna de la guerra. I wish you the peace of
      mind, most royal couplement!                        *Exit.*
530 *King.* Here is like to be a good presence of Worthies. He
      presents Hector of Troy; the swain, Pompey the Great;
      the parish curate, Alexander; Armado's page, Hercules;
      the pedant, Judas Maccabaeus:
      And if these four Worthies in their first show thrive,
535  These four will change habits and present the other five.
      *Berowne.* There is five in the first show.
      *King.* You are deceivèd, 'tis not so.
      *Berowne.* The pedant, the braggart, the hedge-priest, the
      fool, and the boy —
540  Abate throw at novum, and the whole world again
      Cannot pick out five such, take each one in his vein.
      *King.* The ship is under sail, and here she comes amain.

*Enter [Costard armed, for] Pompey.*

*Costard.* 'I Pompey am —'

528 *fortuna . . . guerra* fortunes of war  529 *couplement* couple  530 *presence* appearance, showing  535 *habits* costumes  538 *hedge-priest* (term of contempt for clergyman with no regular stipend)  540 *Abate* barring *throw at novum* lucky throw (in the dice game of novum or nines)  541 *vein* i.e. characteristic manner

*Boyet.*                    You lie, you are not he.

*Costard.* 'I Pompey am —'

*Boyet.*                    With libbard's head on knee.

*Berowne.* Well said, old mocker. I must needs be friends
 with thee.                                                    545

*Costard.* 'I Pompey am, Pompey surnamed the Big —'

*Dumaine.* The 'Great.'

*Costard.* It is 'Great,' sir — 'Pompey surnamed the Great;
 That oft in field, with targe and shield, did make my foe
  to sweat,
 And travelling along this coast, I here am come by chance,  550
 And lay my arms before the legs of this sweet lass of
  France.'
 If your ladyship would say, 'Thanks, Pompey,' I had
  done.

*Princess.* Great thanks, great Pompey.

*Costard.* 'Tis not so much worth; but I hope I was perfect.
 I made a little fault in 'Great.'                            555

*Berowne.* My hat to a halfpenny, Pompey proves the best
 Worthy.

*Enter [Nathaniel, the] Curate, for Alexander.*

*Nathaniel.* 'When in the world I lived, I was the world's
 commander;
 By east, west, north, and south, I spread my conquering
  might;
 My scutcheon plain declares that I am Alisander —'          560

*Boyet.* Your nose says, no, you are not; for it stands too
 right.

---

544 *libbard's* leopard's (a reference to the insignia of Pompey, here presumably worn on the knee)  549 *targe* shield  554 *perfect* word-perfect
561 *right* (a reference to Alexander's wry neck which inclined his head to the left)

*Berowne.* Your nose smells 'no' in this, most tender-smelling
   knight.

*Princess.* The conqueror is dismayed. Proceed, good Alexander.

*Nathaniel.* 'When in the world I lived, I was the world's
   commander —'                                    *[He falters.]*

565 *Boyet.* Most true, 'tis right — you were so, Alisander.

*Berowne.* Pompey the Great —

*Costard.* Your servant, and Costard.

*Berowne.* Take away the conqueror, take away Alisander.

*Costard. [to Nathaniel]* O, sir, you have overthrown Ali-
570  sander the conqueror! You will be scraped out of the
   painted cloth for this. Your lion that holds his pollaxe sitting on a close-stool will be given to Ajax. He will be the
   ninth Worthy. A conqueror, and afeard to speak? Run
   away for shame, Alisander. *[Nathaniel retires.]* There, an 't
575  shall please you, a foolish mild man; an honest man, look
   you, and soon dashed. He is a marvellous good neighbor,
   faith, and a very good bowler; but for Alisander — alas,
   you see how 'tis — a little o'erparted. But there are Worthies a-coming will speak their mind in some other sort.

580 *Princess.* Stand aside, good Pompey.

*Enter [Holofernes, the] Pedant, for Judas, and [Moth,]
   the Boy, for Hercules.*

*Holofernes.* 'Great Hercules is presented by this imp,
   Whose club killed Cerberus, that three-headed canus;
   And when he was a babe, a child, a shrimp,
   Thus did he strangle serpents in his manus.

571 *painted cloth* (wall hanging picturing the Nine Worthies)  571–72 *lion
. . . close-stool* (Alexander's insignia pictured a lion seated in a chair and
holding a battleaxe)  572 *close-stool* seat in a privy  *Ajax* legendary Greek
chieftain (with play on 'a jakes'—privy)  578 *o'erparted* i.e. given too hard
a rôle  581 *imp* shoot, boy  582 *canus* dog  584 *manus* hands

Quoniam he seemeth in minority,                                    585
Ergo I come with this apology.'
Keep some state in thy exit, and vanish.            *Exit Boy.*
'Judas I am —'
*Dumaine.* A Judas?
*Holofernes.* Not Iscariot, sir.                                   590
'Judas I am, ycleped Maccabaeus.'
*Dumaine.* Judas Maccabaeus clipt is plain Judas.
*Berowne.* A kissing traitor. How, art thou proved Judas?
*Holofernes.* 'Judas I am —'
*Dumaine.* The more shame for you, Judas.                          595
*Holofernes.* What mean you, sir?
*Boyet.* To make Judas hang himself.
*Holofernes.* Begin, sir; you are my elder.
*Berowne.* Well followed: Judas was hanged on an elder.
*Holofernes.* I will not be put out of countenance.               600
*Berowne.* Because thou hast no face.
*Holofernes.* What is this?
*Boyet.* A cittern-head.
*Dumaine.* The head of a bodkin.
*Berowne.* A death's face in a ring.                               605
*Longaville.* The face of an old Roman coin, scarce seen.
*Boyet.* The pommel of Caesar's falchion.
*Dumaine.* The carved-bone face on a flask.
*Berowne.* Saint George's half-cheek in a brooch.
*Dumaine.* Ay, and in a brooch of lead.                            610

---

585 *Quoniam* since  586 *Ergo* therefore  587 *state* dignity  589 *A Judas*
i.e. a traitor  591 *ycleped* called  *Maccabaeus* (Hebrew warrior)  592 *clipt*
shortened  593 *How* how now  598 *you ... elder* i.e. you are so wise  603
*cittern* cithern, guitar  604 *bodkin* small dagger  605 *face* head  *ring*
(death's-head ring worn as a memento mori)  607 *falchion* sword  608
*flask* i.e. engraved horn flask  609 *half-cheek* profile  610–11 *brooch ...
toothdrawer* (i.e. an inferior badge bearing insignia, possibly jawbones, of an
inferior occupation)

*Berowne.* Ay, and worn in the cap of a toothdrawer.

And now forward, for we have put thee in countenance.

*Holofernes.* You have put me out of countenance.

*Berowne.* False. We have given thee faces.

615 *Holofernes.* But you have outfaced them all.

*Berowne.* An thou wert a lion, we would do so.

*Boyet.* Therefore as he is (an ass), let him go.

And so adieu, sweet Jude. Nay, why dost thou stay?

*Dumaine.* For the latter end of his name.

*Berowne.* For the ass to the Jude? Give it him. Jud-as,
620     away!

*Holofernes.* This is not generous, not gentle, not humble.

*Boyet.* A light for Monsieur Judas! It grows dark, he may
    stumble.                              *[Holofernes retires.]*

*Princess.* Alas, poor Maccabaeus, how hath he been baited!

*Enter [Armado, the] Braggart, [for Hector].*

*Berowne.* Hide thy head, Achilles! Here comes Hector in
625     arms.

*Dumaine.* Though my mocks come home by me, I will now
    be merry.

*King.* Hector was but a Troyan in respect of this.

*Boyet.* But is this Hector?

630 *King.* I think Hector was not so clean-timbered.

*Longaville.* His leg is too big for Hector's.

*Dumaine.* More calf, certain.

*Boyet.* No; he is best indued in the small.

*Berowne.* This cannot be Hector.

612 *put . . . countenance* i.e. portrayed you   615 *outfaced* abashed   621
*humble* i.e. considerate, the reverse of arrogant   624 *Hide . . . Achilles*
i.e. beware, or skulk in your tent, Achilles (the Greek champion who de-
feated the Trojan Hector)   626 *by me* to me, to afflict me   628 *Troyan* (1)
roisterer (2) Trojan   *respect of* comparison with   630 *clean-timbered* clean-
limbed, well-built   633 *indued . . . small* endowed in the ankle

*Dumaine.* He's a god or a painter; for he makes faces.                635

*Armado.* 'The armipotent Mars, of lances the almighty,
 Gave Hector a gift —'

*Dumaine.* A gilt nutmeg.

*Berowne.* A lemon.

*Longaville.* Stuck with cloves.                640

*Dumaine.* No, cloven.

*Armado.* Peace!

 'The armipotent Mars, of lances the almighty,
 Gave Hector a gift, the heir of Ilion;
 A man so breathed that certain he would fight, yea        645
 From morn till night, out of his pavilion.
 I am that flower —'

*Dumaine.*                   That mint.

*Longaville.*                         That columbine.

*Armado.* Sweet Lord Longaville, rein thy tongue.

*Longaville.* I must rather give it the rein, for it runs against
 Hector.                645

*Dumaine.* Ay, and Hector's a greyhound.

*Armado.* The sweet war-man is dead and rotten. Sweet
 chucks, beat not the bones of the buried. When he
 breathed, he was a man. But I will forward with my
 device. *[to the Princess]* Sweet royalty, bestow on me the   655
 sense of hearing.    *Berowne steps forth [to prompt Costard].*

*Princess.* Speak, brave Hector; we are much delighted.

*Armado.* I do adore thy sweet Grace's slipper.

*Boyet.* *[aside to Dumaine]* Loves her by the foot.

---

636 *armipotent* powerful in arms  638–40 *gilt nutmeg . . . cloves* (nutmegs,
sometimes gilded, were used to flavor ale and wine, as were lemons stuck
with cloves; the latter were also valued for their scent: the joking is obscure but relates to Armado's artificiality)  644 *Ilion* Troy  645 *so
breathed* of such strong lungs, lasting power  646 *pavilion* jousting-tent
648 *rein* curb  649 *runs against* (1) tilts against (2) races  651 *Hector's a
greyhound* i.e. 'Hector' is a term for a greyhound

660 *Dumaine.* [*aside to Boyet*] He may not by the yard.

*Armado.* 'This Hector far surmounted Hannibal —'

*Costard.* The party is gone. Fellow Hector, she is gone. She is two months on her way.

*Armado.* What meanest thou?

665 *Costard.* Faith, unless you play the honest Troyan, the poor wench is cast away. She's quick; the child brags in her belly already. 'Tis yours.

*Armado.* Dost thou infamonize me among potentates? Thou shalt die.

670 *Costard.* Then shall Hector be whipped for Jaquenetta that is quick by him, and hanged for Pompey that is dead by him.

*Dumaine.* Most rare Pompey!

*Boyet.* Renowned Pompey!

675 *Berowne.* Greater than great. Great, great, great Pompey! Pompey the Huge!

*Dumaine.* Hector trembles.

*Berowne.* Pompey is moved. More Ates, more Ates! Stir them on! stir them on!

680 *Dumaine.* Hector will challenge him.

*Berowne.* Ay, if 'a have no more man's blood in his belly than will sup a flea.

*Armado.* By the north pole, I do challenge thee.

*Costard.* I will not fight with a pole, like a northern man.

685 I'll slash; I'll do it by the sword. I bepray you, let me borrow my arms again.

*Dumaine.* Room for the incensed Worthies!

*Costard.* I'll do it in my shirt.

*Dumaine.* Most resolute Pompey!

---

660 *yard* (slang for 'phallus')   666 *quick* pregnant   668 *infamonize* infamize, slander   678 *Ates* (underworld spirits of discord)   681 *blood . . . belly* i.e. courage   684 *northern man* border ruffian

*Moth.* Master, let me take you a button-hole lower. Do you 690
   not see, Pompey is uncasing for the combat? What mean
   you? You will lose your reputation.

*Armado.* Gentlemen and soldiers, pardon me. I will not
   combat in my shirt.

*Dumaine.* You may not deny it. Pompey hath made the 695
   challenge.

*Armado.* Sweet bloods, I both may and will.

*Berowne.* What reason have you for 't?

*Armado.* The naked truth of it is, I have no shirt. I go woolward for penance.                                        700

*Boyet.* True, and it was enjoined him in Rome for want of
   linen; since when, I'll be sworn he wore none but a dish-
   clout of Jaquenetta's, and that 'a wears next his heart for a
   favor.

*Enter a Messenger, Monsieur Marcade.*

*Marcade.* God save you, madam.                            705

*Princess.* Welcome, Marcade;
   But that thou interrupt'st our merriment.

*Marcade.* I am sorry, madam, for the news I bring
   Is heavy in my tongue. The king your father —

*Princess.* Dead, for my life!                             710

*Marcade.* Even so. My tale is told.

*Berowne.* Worthies, away! The scene begins to cloud.

*Armado.* For mine own part, I breathe free breath. I have
   seen the day of wrong through the little hole of discretion,
   and I will right myself like a soldier.     *Exeunt Worthies.* 715

*King.* How fares your Majesty?

690 *take . . . lower* (1) take you down to your underwear (2) humiliate
you (proverbial) 691 *uncasing* undressing 699–700 *woolward for penance* i.e. with wool next to the skin to discipline the flesh 713–14 *I have
. . . discretion* i.e. I have caught on to the fact that I am abused ('to see day
through a little hole' was proverbial for 'to be no fool')

*Princess.* Boyet, prepare. I will away to-night.
*King.* Madam, not so. I do beseech you, stay.
*Princess.* Prepare, I say. I thank you, gracious lords,
720  For all your fair endeavors, and entreat,
      Out of a new-sad soul, that you vouchsafe
      In your rich wisdom to excuse or hide
      The liberal opposition of our spirits,
      If over-boldly we have borne ourselves
725  In the converse of breath: your gentleness
      Was guilty of it. Farewell, worthy lord.
      A heavy heart bears not a humble tongue;
      Excuse me so, coming too short of thanks
      For my great suit so easily obtained.
730 *King.* The extreme parts of time extremely forms
      All causes to the purpose of his speed,
      And often, at his very loose, decides
      That which long process could not arbitrate.
      And though the mourning brow of progeny
735  Forbid the smiling courtesy of love
      The holy suit which fain it would convince,
      Yet, since love's argument was first on foot,
      Let not the cloud of sorrow justle it
      From what it purposed; since to wail friends lost
740  Is not by much so wholesome-profitable
      As to rejoice at friends but newly found.
*Princess.* I understand you not. My griefs are double.

722 *hide* i.e. ignore  723 *liberal* too free  725 *converse of breath* exchange
of conversation  *gentleness* courtesy  726 *guilty of* responsible for  727
*humble* i.e. adapted to courtly civilities  728 *so* therefore  729 *suit* i.e.
the property claims (which Navarre has evidently granted)  730–31 *The
. . . speed* i.e. final moments enforce quick decisions  732 *his* i.e. time's
*loose* slipping away, release (archery term)  734 *progeny* i.e. child of the
deceased  736 *suit . . . convince* i.e. the case it would like to make  742
*double* i.e. her failure to understand is an additional grief (?)

*Berowne.* Honest plain words best pierce the ear of
    grief;
  And by these badges understand the king.
  For your fair sakes have we neglected time,        745
  Played foul play with our oaths. Your beauty, ladies,
  Hath much deformed us, fashioning our humors
  Even to the opposèd end of our intents;
  And what in us hath seemed ridiculous –
  As love is full of unbefitting strains,        750
  All wanton as a child, skipping and vain,
  Formed by the eye and therefore, like the eye,
  Full of straying shapes, of habits and of forms,
  Varying in subjects as the eye doth roll
  To every varied object in his glance;        755
  Which parti-coated presence of loose love
  Put on by us, if, in your heavenly eyes,
  Have misbecomed our oaths and gravities,
  Those heavenly eyes that look into these faults
  Suggested us to make. Therefore, ladies,       760
  Our love being yours, the error that love makes
  Is likewise yours. We to ourselves prove false,
  By being once false for ever to be true
  To those that make us both – fair ladies, you.
  And even that falsehood, in itself a sin,       765
  Thus purifies itself and turns to grace.

*Princess.* We have received your letters, full of love;
  Your favors, the ambassadors of love;
  And in our maiden council rated them
  At courtship, pleasant jest, and courtesy,       770

744 *badges* tokens, testimony  745 *neglected time* i.e. disregarded proper
occasion  748 *Even . . . intents* quite contrary to our intentions  750
*strains* impulses  753 *habits* demeanors  756 *parti-coated presence* i.e. jesting
appearance  758 *misbecomed* been unbecoming to  760 *Suggested . . . make*
tempted us to make them  769 *rated* evaluated  770 *At* at no more than

As bombast and as lining to the time.
But more devout than this in our respects
Have we not been, and therefore met your loves
In their own fashion, like a merriment.

*Dumaine.* Our letters, madam, showed much more than
775      jest.

*Longaville.* So did our looks.

*Rosaline.*                    We did not quote them so.

*King.* Now, at the latest minute of the hour,
Grant us your loves.

*Princess.*                    A time, methinks, too short
To make a world-without-end bargain in.
780      No, no, my lord, your Grace is perjured much,
Full of dear guiltiness; and therefore this —
If for my love (as there is no such cause)
You will do aught, this shall you do for me:
Your oath I will not trust, but go with speed
785      To some forlorn and naked hermitage,
Remote from all the pleasures of the world;
There stay until the twelve celestial signs
Have brought about the annual reckoning.
If this austere insociable life
790      Change not your offer made in heat of blood;
If frosts and fasts, hard lodging and thin weeds,
Nip not the gaudy blossoms of your love,
But that it bear this trial, and last love;
Then, at the expiration of the year,
795      Come challenge me, challenge me by these deserts,

771 *bombast . . . time* i.e. way to fill in time   *bombast, lining* padding   772
*devout* serious   *respects* consideration   776 *quote* interpret   781 *dear*
grievous   782 *such cause* i.e. reason why you should   783 *aught* anything
(i.e. everything)   787 *signs* i.e. of the zodiac (the months)   791 *weeds*
garments   793 *that* so long as   *last* remain   795 *these deserts* i.e. demonstrated merit

And, by this virgin palm now kissing thine,
I will be thine; and till that instant, shut
My woeful self up in a mourning house,
Raining the tears of lamentation
For the remembrance of my father's death.            800
If this thou do deny, let our hands part;
Neither intitled in the other's heart.

*King.* If this, or more than this, I would deny,
To flatter up these powers of mine with rest,
The sudden hand of death close up mine eye!           805
Hence hermit then — my heart is in thy breast.

[*Berowne.* And what to me, my love? and what to me?

*Rosaline.* You must be purgèd too; your sins are racked,
You are attaint with faults and perjury;
Therefore, if you my favor mean to get,              810
A twelvemonth shall you spend, and never rest,
But seek the weary beds of people sick.]

*Dumaine.* But what to me, my love? but what to me?
A wife?

*Katharine.*        A beard, fair health, and honesty;
With three-fold love I wish you all these three.      815

*Dumaine.* O, shall I say 'I thank you, gentle wife'?

*Katharine.* Not so, my lord. A twelvemonth and a
day
I'll mark no words that smooth-faced wooers say.
Come when the king doth to my lady come;
Then, if I have much love, I'll give you some.        820

*Dumaine.* I'll serve thee true and faithfully till then.

*Katharine.* Yet swear not, lest ye be forsworn again.

*Longaville.* What says Maria?

804 *flatter up* pamper  806 *hermit* i.e. as a hermit  807–12 *Berowne . . .
sick* (a passage probably marked for excision in the manuscript since another version appears below, ll. 827 ff.)  808 *racked* stretched out

*Maria.*                          At the twelvemonth's end
   I'll change my black gown for a faithful friend.
825 *Longaville.* I'll stay with patience, but the time is long.
   *Maria.* The liker you — few taller are so young.
   *Berowne.* Studies my lady? Mistress, look on me.
     Behold the window of my heart, mine eye,
     What humble suit attends thy answer there.
830   Impose some service on me for thy love.
   *Rosaline.* Oft have I heard of you, my Lord Berowne,
     Before I saw you; and the world's large tongue
     Proclaims you for a man replete with mocks,
     Full of comparisons and wounding flouts,
835   Which you on all estates will execute
     That lie within the mercy of your wit.
     To weed this wormwood from your fructful brain,
     And therewithal to win me, if you please —
     Without the which I am not to be won —
840   You shall this twelvemonth term from day to day
     Visit the speechless sick, and still converse
     With groaning wretches; and your task shall be
     With all the fierce endeavor of your wit
     To enforce the painèd impotent to smile.
845 *Berowne.* To move wild laughter in the throat of death?
     It cannot be; it is impossible:
     Mirth cannot move a soul in agony.
   *Rosaline.* Why, that's the way to choke a gibing spirit,
     Whose influence is begot of that loose grace
850   Which shallow laughing hearers give to fools.
     A jest's prosperity lies in the ear

825 *stay* wait  826 *liker* more like  834 *comparisons* i.e. similes of a de-
risive sort  *flouts* gibes  835 *estates* sorts of people  837 *fructful* fruitful
844 *painèd impotent* those prostrated by suffering  849 *loose grace* slack
approval

Of him that hears it, never in the tongue
Of him that makes it. Then, if sickly ears,
Deafed with the clamors of their own dear groans,
Will hear your idle scorns, continue then,                     855
And I will have you and that fault withal;
But if they will not, throw away that spirit,
And I shall find you empty of that fault,
Right joyful of your reformation.

*Berowne.* A twelvemonth? Well, befall what will befall,   860
   I'll jest a twelvemonth in an hospital.

*Princess.* *[to the King]* Ay, sweet my lord; and so I take my
   leave.

*King.* No, madam; we will bring you on your way.

*Berowne.* Our wooing doth not end like an old play;
   Jack hath not Jill. These ladies' courtesy                  865
   Might well have made our sport a comedy.

*King.* Come, sir, it wants a twelvemonth and a day,
   And then 'twill end.

*Berowne.*          That's too long for a play.

*Enter [Armado, the] Braggart.*

*Armado.* Sweet majesty, vouchsafe me —

*Princess.* Was not that Hector?                               870

*Dumaine.* The worthy knight of Troy.

*Armado.* I will kiss thy royal finger, and take leave. I am a
   votary; I have vowed to Jaquenetta to hold the plough
   for her sweet love three year. But, most esteemed greatness, will you hear the dialogue that the two learned men 875
   have compiled in praise of the owl and the cuckoo? It
   should have followed in the end of our show.

854 *dear* grievous  856 *withal* in addition  865 *courtesy* polite compliance
873 *hold the plough* i.e. toil at husbandry  875 *dialogue* debate

*King.* Call them forth quickly; we will do so.
*Armado.* Holla! approach.

*Enter all.*

880   This side is Hiems, Winter; this Ver, the Spring; the one
      maintained by the owl, th' other by the cuckoo. Ver,
      begin.

The Song.

[*Spring.*]    When daisies pied and violets blue
                   And lady-smocks all silver-white
885            And cuckoo-buds of yellow hue
                   Do paint the meadows with delight,
               The cuckoo then, on every tree,
               Mocks married men; for thus sings he,
                                           Cuckoo;
890            Cuckoo, cuckoo: O, word of fear,
               Unpleasing to a married ear!

               When shepherds pipe on oaten straws,
                   And merry larks are ploughmen's clocks,
               When turtles tread, and rooks, and daws,
895                And maidens bleach their summer smocks,
               The cuckoo then, on every tree,
                   Mocks married men; for thus sings he,
                                           Cuckoo;
               Cuckoo, cuckoo: O, word of fear,
900            Unpleasing to a married ear!

884 *lady-smocks* cuckoo-flowers (cardamine pratensis)   885 *cuckoo-buds*
buttercups (ranunculus bulbosus)   892 *oaten straws* pipes made of oat-
reeds   893 *ploughmen's clocks* (since ploughmen 'rise with the lark')   894
*turtles tread* turtledoves mate

*Winter.*    When icicles hang by the wall,
    And Dick the shepherd blows his nail,
And Tom bears logs into the hall,
    And milk comes frozen home in pail,
When blood is nipped, and ways be foul,    905
Then nightly sings the staring owl,
                        Tu-who;
Tu-whit, tu-who: a merry note,
While greasy Joan doth keel the pot.

When all aloud the wind doth blow,    910
    And coughing drowns the parson's saw,
And birds sit brooding in the snow,
    And Marian's nose looks red and raw,
When roasted crabs hiss in the bowl,
Then nightly sings the staring owl,    915
                        Tu-who;
Tu-whit, tu-who: a merry note,
While greasy Joan doth keel the pot.

*[Armado.]* The words of Mercury are harsh after the songs
    of Apollo. [You, that way: we, this way.    920

Separation, not    *Exeunt omnes.]*
Reunion! Not permanent sep.,
    tho'.

---

902 *nail* fingernails   909 *keel* stir and skim (to prevent boiling over)
911 *saw* moral maxim   914 *crabs* crab-apples   919 *Mercury* messenger of
the gods (but associated with clever sophistry)   920 *Apollo* Greek god
(associated with song and beauty)

# Appendix: List of Emendations

Below are listed all substantive departures from the quarto of 1598. The adopted reading is given in italics, followed by the reading in the quarto.

I, i, 62 *feast* fast   104 *an* any   126-129 *A . . . devise* (joined in Q with Longaville's preceding speech)   129 *possibly* possible

I, ii, 13 *epitheton* apethaton   95 *blushing* blush-in   135 *Dull* (assigned in Q to Costard)

II, i, 32 *Importunes* Importuous   34 *visaged* visage   40 *Maria* 1 Lady   44 *parts* peerless   53 *Maria* Lady   56 *Katharine* 2 Lady   64 *Rosaline* 3 Lady   88 *unpeopled* unpeeled   99 *it; will* it will   114-25 *Rosaline* Katharine   143 *On* One   193 *Katharine* Rosaline   208 *Rosaline* Katharine   252 *Rosaline* Lady   253 *Maria* Lady 2   254 *Katharine* Lady 3   255, 256 *Rosaline* Lady

III, i, 12 *as if* if   13 *through the* through:   16 *thin-belly* thinbellies   21 *note—do you note—men that* note: do you note men that   24 *penny* pen   65-66 *the mail* thee male   169 *senior-junior* Signior Junios   179 *clock* cloake   193 *sue* shue

IV, i, 6 *On* Ore   69 *saw* see   70 *saw* see   74 *king's* king   107 *suitor . . . suitor* shooter . . . shooter   129 *hit it* hit   135 *pin is* in   143 *o' th' t'one* 'ath toothen

IV, ii, 35 *Dictynna . . . Dictynna* Dictisima . . . Dictisima   36 *Dictynna* dictima   49 *call I* called   58 *sores—O sore l!* sores o sorell:   63 *Holofernes* Nathaniel   67 *pia mater* primater   68 *in whom* whom   70 *Nathaniel* Holofernes   74-89 *Holofernes* Nathaniel   76 *sapit* sapis   92-93 *Venechia . . . prechia* vemchie, vencha, que non te unde, que non te perreche   115 *apostrophus* apostraphas   116 *canzonet* cangenet   116-23 *Here . . . you* (assigned in Q to Nathaniel)   126-30 *I will . . . Berowne* (assigned in Q to Nathaniel)   129 *writing* written   131 *Sir Nathaniel* Sir Holofernes   151 *ben* bien

IV, iii, 44 *King* Longaville   48 *triumviry* triumphery   88 *I mine* mine   103 *Wished* wish   107 *thorn* throne   125 *o'erheard* ore-hard   175 *like you* like   243 *wood* word   254 *and usurping* usurping   354 *authors* author   378 *Allons, allons* Alone, alone

V, i, 9 *hominem* hominum 24 *insanie* infamie 26 *Deo bone* Deo, bene 27 *Bone . . . Priscian* Bome boon for boon prescian 55 *venew* vene we 62 *manu* unum 89 *importunate* importunt 98 *secrecy* secretie 106 *Sir Nathaniel* Sir Holofernes 108 *rend'red* rended *assistance* assistants 138 *Allons* alone

V, ii, 17 *ha'* a *a grandam* grandam 28 *cure . . . care* care . . . cure 43 *pencils, ho!* pensalls, How? 53 *pearls* pearl 65 *hests* device 74 *wantonness* wantons be 80 *stabbed* stable 89 *sycamore* siccamone 148 *her* his 152 *ne'er* ere 159 *Boyet* Berowne 161 *—backs—* backs 217 *The . . . it* (assigned in Q to Rosaline) 243-56 *Katharine* Maria 298 *vailing* varling 310 *run o'er the* runs o'er 375 *wit* wits 464 *zany* saine 483 *manage* nuage 514 *least* best 528 *de la guerra* delaguar 562 *this* his 638 *gilt* gift 679 *on!* stir or stir 720 *entreat* entreat: 768 *the ambassadors* ambassadors 772 *this in our* this our 776 *quote* cote 797 *instant* instance 802 *intitled* intiled 806 *hermit* herrite 808 *too,* to 814 *A wife* (included in following speech in Q) 884, 885 (these lines transposed in Q) 905 *foul* full 907, 916 *Tu-who* (omitted in Q) 919-20 *Armado . . . omnes* (The quarto text concludes with 'The words of Mercury are harsh after the songs of Apollo' printed in larger type below the song. The first folio adds the speech prefix, together with 'You, that way: we, this way. Exeunt omnes.' Thus the words of the quarto are made, if they were not so already, an integral part of the play.)

*Details of the
Pelican Shakespeare and
other Penguin books
follow.*

# THE PELICAN SHAKESPEARE

*General Editor: Alfred Harbage*

## Tragedies

| | |
|---|---|
| Edited by Maynard Mack | ANTONY AND CLEOPATRA |
| Harry Levin | CORIOLANUS |
| Willard Farnham | HAMLET |
| S. F. Johnson | JULIUS CAESAR |
| Alfred Harbage | KING LEAR |
| Alfred Harbage | MACBETH |
| Gerald E. Bentley | OTHELLO |
| John E. Hankins | ROMEO AND JULIET |
| Charlton Hinman | TIMON OF ATHENS* |

## Comedies

| | |
|---|---|
| Jonas Barish | ALL'S WELL THAT ENDS WELL* |
| Ralph Sargent | AS YOU LIKE IT |
| Paul A. Jorgensen | THE COMEDY OF ERRORS* |
| Robert B. Heilman | CYMBELINE* |
| Alfred Harbage | LOVE'S LABOR'S LOST* |
| R. C. Bald | MEASURE FOR MEASURE |
| Brents Stirling | THE MERCHANT OF VENICE |
| Fredson T. Bowers | THE MERRY WIVES OF WINDSOR* |
| Madeleine Doran | A MIDSUMMER NIGHT'S DREAM |
| Josephine Waters Bennett | MUCH ADO ABOUT NOTHING |
| Richard Hosley | THE TAMING OF THE SHREW* |
| Northrop Frye | THE TEMPEST |
| Virgil Whitaker | TROILUS AND CRESSIDA |
| Charles Prouty | TWELFTH NIGHT |
| Berners Jackson | TWO GENTLEMEN OF VERONA* |
| Baldwin Maxwell | THE WINTER'S TALE |

## Histories and Poems

| | |
|---|---|
| M. A. Shaaber | HENRY IV, PART I |
| Allan Chester | HENRY IV, PART II |
| Louis B. Wright and V. Freund | HENRY V |
| Irving Ribner | KING JOHN |
| Matthew Black | RICHARD II |
| G. Blakemore Evans | RICHARD III |
| Douglas Bush | THE SONNETS |

*In preparation

# PLAYS BY BERNARD SHAW

*The following plays are published
in Penguin editions. Each play has the
complete text and the
author's preface*

# CHAUCER: THE CANTERBURY TALES

*A Modern Version By*
*Nevill Coghill*

This is the first English work to be included in the Penguin Classics series of modern translations. When it was published it was widely acclaimed as a means of bringing Chaucer to thousands of people who would never have read him otherwise. Reviewers were quick to realize that Mr Coghill, who is a fellow of Exeter College, Oxford, was the right person to have attempted the task.

*Punch* offered very high praise by saying ' . . . this translation will remain a beloved classic until the language changes again sufficiently to call for another renaissance'. *The Manchester Guardian* found that 'Mr Coghill has achieved his aim that his translation should be considered as a poem and not as a crib'. And the most enthusiastic welcome came from *The Times Educational Supplement* which said, 'Altogether Mr Coghill's achievement is remarkable. He has been almost consistently successful and his practice carries out his theory and intentions. The bland, humorous, observing, and courtly spirit that informs the original is somehow preserved in a different idiom'.

SPECIALLY WRITTEN FOR PENGUINS

# THE GREEK MYTHS

## *Robert Graves*

Not for over a century, since Smith's *Dictionary of Classical Mythology* first appeared, has the attempt been made to provide for the English reader a complete 'mythology,' in the sense of a retelling in modern terms of the Greek tales of gods and heroes. In the two volumes of this book Robert Graves, whose combination of classical scholarship and anthropological competence has already been so brilliantly demonstrated in *The White Goddess* and *Hercules, My Shipmate,* and his other novels, supplies the need. In nearly two hundred sections, it covers the Creation myths, the legends of the birth and lives of the great Olympians, the Theseus, Oedipus, and Heracles cycles, the Argonaut voyage, the tale of Troy, and much else.

All the scattered elements of each myth have been assembled into a harmonious narrative, which notes also many variants which may help to determine its ritual or historical meaning. Full references to the classical sources, and copious indexes, make the book as valuable to the scholar as to the general reader; and a full commentary to each myth explains and interprets the classical version in the light of to-day's archaeological and anthropological knowledge.